THE ETHNICITY OF NEURONS:
NATIONALISM A SELF-ESTEEM OF FOOLS

THE ETHNICITY OF NEURONS:
NATIONALISM A SELF-ESTEEM OF FOOLS

DARKO POZDER

To order additional copies of this book, contact:
Xlibris
AU TFN: 1 800 844 927 (Toll Free inside Australia)
AU Local: (02) 8310 8187 (+61 2 8310 8187 from outside Australia)
www.Xlibris.com.au
Orders@Xlibris.com.au
850202

CONTENTS

This book is dedicated to every and each person who died as a consequence of the war or any other conflict caused by a human psychological error called nationalism. Sadly, many people will lose their lives in the future due to this horrible phenomenon which I like to call mind cancer. A strong need for nationalism is a sign of low self-esteem, insecurity, primitivism, stupidity, external locus of control, delusion, irrationality, anxiety, and fear rather than good and stable psychological health and well-being. Nationalism is nothing less than psychological self-destruction. When one goes beyond the need for identity, a strong sense of security and well-being often demonstrates confidence and self-control resulting in showing empathy and trust in others. Trust and empathy unite our societies while fear, low self-esteem, anxiety, and primitivism as well as the illusion of control result in new nations, new religions, and new states and countries, rarely without bloody wars and human suffering.

To conclude, nationalism is nothing more than the self-esteem of fools, a very dangerous cognitive or psychological error created by our faulty thinking patterns. So far it caused nothing more than horrible, irreversible, and devastating damage to the human race. Einstein was wrong when he said that nationalism was just an infantile disease. In my eyes, nationalism is not only an illusion with no future, it is cancer to the human race. I am shocked by the fact that every second two people die from war conflicts around the globe while cancer takes a life every fourteen seconds. Nationalism is constantly promoted and on the rise. It is even twenty-eight times deadlier than cancer. As a rational human being, I felt the urge to write this book which will hopefully create an impact on humanity and save the lives of many. As mentioned earlier in my previous books, the fight against nature is mission impossible. However, we all must give our best in that regard. In Hemingway's novel, *The Old man and the Sea*, an old fisherman Santiago didn't give up fighting nature, and I think we should all follow his steps at all costs.

If I have to describe an extreme mix of malignant
narcissism, ignorance, aggression and sadism in a single
word I will have no choice then call it nationalism.

—Darko Pozder

Nationalism is not only an illusion with no
future, it is a cancer to the human race.

—Darko Pozder

Nationalism is a low self-esteem of fools.

—Darko Pozder

CHAPTER I

Introduction

More often than not, the terms nationalism and patriotism have been used interchangeably. In this sense, they have been used to refer to love and loyalty for one's country. While the terms could connote the perceived meanings, they have been used in different ways by various theorists and national leaders, bringing more confusion than an understanding of what the terms mean and how they apply to the lives of leaders and their followers over time[1]. The words were once considered synonyms even if they had been taken on different connotations. The terms nationalism and patriotism refer to an individual's love for one's country with the values upon which those feelings are based differing between the two terms.

Researchers and philosophers attribute patriotism to positive feelings for one's country and the ability of citizens to embrace values that enhance peace and stability within the nation, such as freedom, justice, and equality. However, the notion that one's country is superior to all others has been linked to feelings of nationalism. This implies disdain and mistrust of other nations, which could result in conflicts that could be harmful to others[2]. The language of nationalism seems to have been coined in the eighteenth century within the European region to reinforce elements of culture, language, ethnic unity, and homogeneity of people[3]. Nationalists felt that nationalism was adversely affected by cultural contamination, heterogeneity within the nation, impurity across countries, and political, social, and intellectual disunion.

On the other hand, patriots felt that patriotism was greatly affected by despotism, tyranny, oppression, and corruption. This implies that the two terms only loosely translate to the love for one's country, yet there are more differences to it than their simple meanings. The implications are so diverse that leaders often exhibit nationalistic or patriotic interests to gain citizens' support within and across national boundaries.

Patriotism

Patriotism is derived from *patria*, meaning country. Patriots are, therefore, citizens who show the love of a country coupled with the readiness to sacrifice for its good [4]. In the past, this loyalty and allegiance to one's country were common among Spartans of classical antiquity. These refer to a warrior society in ancient Greece, reaching its power following the defeat of rival city-states in Athens. The community's culture was founded on loyalty to the states and military services. Spartans were citizens in the strict sense of the term. They shared identity with those within their nations and those related through blood and a sense of belonging to the community. Training in patriotism was done to children when they were still young [5]. Children were recruited and trained to be soldiers. Their readiness to participate in fights was exemplified by the war with the Persians resulting in the death of three hundred Spartan soldiers in 480 BC.

Patriotism is a term linked to the virtue of membership or belongingness. To participate in such relations, one has to form loyalty to an organisation or nation with value expectations related to such membership. This means that citizens are expected to express devotion to their countries, live to the expectations of the leaders, and uphold values that elevate their nations. Patriotism denotes a unique loyalty linked to an individual's membership in a country or state. Patriotism also covers a sense of personal identification of individuals in the nation. Here, individuals express their sense of identification and belongingness by showing concern, welfare, and well-being of the state [6]. It also covers the readiness of citizens to make sacrifices for the country's defence and welfare. Patriotism has also been cited to protect the citizen's sense of morality, providing the foundation around which specific actions and activities are based.

The virtue of patriotism refers to the fondness an individual for their country or place. This kind of love is compared to an individual's love for their mothers. According to the American scholar William Gustin, patriotism denotes a special attachment to a specified political community and not necessarily to an existing form of government [7]. A patriot celebrates what they are born to without passion for the superiority of one nation over others or other forms of being.

Components of patriotism, therefore, lie in the special love an individual feels towards their own country, the sentiment for them to define themselves as belonging to the identified nation, and their ability to express concern and welfare for one's country. According to Nathanson, another crucial feature involves the ability of individuals to make sacrifices in favour of one's country[8]. Patriotism is expressed in nostalgia for an individual's or community's patch of land, the spec closest to one's sense of being, singing the national anthem during a celebration of events, and pride in the county's sportsmanship and independence days or similar occasions. Other aspects refer to the attachment to specific forms of clothing, food, and the expression of gratitude for servicemen and women who dedicate their time to serving the country.

Ideologies do not drive patriotism compared to nationalism based on the ability of patriots to take the successes of others positively and do not involve the same destructive devotion associated with nationalism. One of the scholars in the field defines patriotism as a concept in which individuals show their love to their clime, leaving them free to find fault with what they may be lacking without letting bravado or false claims associated with such perspectives distort realities of associations. Nationalism, on the other hand, provides no room for individuals to accept any faults within their national boundaries and consider others better than them. According to scholars in this field, nationalism requires and impresses upon individuals and communities to outshine all other people, countries, and cultures in all other spheres of live [9]. Here, nationalism pushes its proponents to express and claim the exclusive right of perfection. On the other hand, patriotism accepts the reality of diversity, allowing individuals to place themselves in perspective on what is occurring within and outside their communities.

Patriotism means the love for one's home place and the familiar scenes and things associated with it. It is considered one of the essential human sentiments. The root of patriotism lies in people's capacity to become devoted to people, places, and ways of life that nurture us[10]. Other forms of patriotism cover aspects of indebtedness to the ancestral land and descent of individuals. Covenanted patriotism, as coined by Abraham Lincoln in America, relates to Americans of various races and cultures' ability to bond by political ideas.

Moving away from the definition of the concept, it covers components of an individual's beliefs regarding the merits and achievements of their homeland. It also touches on the need to belong to an identified place of descent and their ability to be considered as part of the broader narrative of an identified location. This calls for the power of individuals to relate to the past and future of a *patria* without the narrow confinement to life and such mundane concerns. It also covers the political and social conditions that affect the nature on which individuals relate to people identified as belonging to the same *patria*[11]. It is worth noting that in modern times, an individual's love is not only related to their country of origin or residence. Love is often expressed to citizens and the state as well to exhibit the general feelings of individuals toward their homeland. In patriotism, *patria* does not only cover the aspects of geographical region. It also covers political elements of where people are located or reside. In modern society, the features of nationalism and patriotism overlap. Hence, the aspects that apply to one can easily be transferred to the other.

Several viewpoints on patriotism have existed and brought controversy since time immemorial. According to Boswell, patriotism is captured in the form of a quote, 'the last refuge of a scoundrel' associated with pretended patriotism[12]. Scholars in the past, as reported in the book The History of English Nationalism quote that 'individuals within nations often seek to associate with those of their own rather than foreigners'. More often than not, people have labelled foreigners as fools. According to Johnson, a patriot is an individual whose public conduct is driven by a love for their country. Individuals searching for power and authority often misuse this term to gain the following and acceptance of most citizens and followers.

According to other researchers in the area, patriotism has also been considered a lively sense of collective responsibility. Individuals here are classified as either moderate or extreme patriots. The two categories are based on the ability of individuals to promote and defend their political, cultural, and economic aspects within their nations and homelands. Extreme patriots are closely related to nationalists because they can go to extreme lengths to express and defend their love for their own countries. On the other hand, moderate patriots recognize universal justice and human solidarity, placing restrictions on what can be done in the name of love and loyalty for one's nation[13]. This type of patriotism, according to Baron, is demonstrated by the way people show a special concern for the welfare of their country even in the performance of their moral duties[14].

Here, a patriot is identified in the manner in which they seek to obtain and show justice to all people within their places of residence. Other critical considerations here include the ability of these individuals to respect rights and show human solidarity at any time and place within societies [14]. Additionally, this kind of patriotism is expressed in the likelihood of individuals exploring the conduct of their own countries while seeking to identify the dark aspects. These individuals also seek ways of remedying such situations to promote a peaceful coexistence of individuals despite their differences in descent and other differentiating factors.

A moral patriot is at the forefront of acknowledging a country's resources, managing them well, and preserving their homeland's natural beauty and historical heritage. Others include the ability of the patriots to promote their cultures and powerful history while promoting their homeland's position through positive influence. Promotion is also done regarding the ability of an identified locality and national boundaries to preserve its moral requirements at both local and international levels. A patriot fights for their homeland to exhibit moral values within local and global limits [15]. A patriot will thus fight for the country to act justly within and outside its border while showing solidarity and empathy towards others even if they are distant and unfamiliar.

The virtue of patriotism pushes citizens to give the best for their country over their self-interests. This aspect is common in wars as citizens, and the military comes together to protect their country from attacks by its enemies. More often than not, people refer to their countries as a *motherland*, indicating love as that directed towards a mother [16]. Here, individuals consider their countries as places where they are nurtured and grow.

Two forms of patriotism exist, each defining how individuals express loyalty and love for their country. Blind patriotism refers to a belonging where an individual accepts policies and actions taken by one's country with unquestioning devotion. Suppose such policies are discriminatory and damaging to specified groups of people, such as minority groups, the blind patriot still supports and adheres to them even if they amount to a violation of human rights. The object of dependency for blind patriotism may change from time to time based on the presenting circumstances. The object may also be different from one society to another. Some of the stated objects of loyalty for blind patriotism could include aspects such as one's country, state, people, concepts, ideologies, and opinions. What remains fixed, however, is the unconditional loyalty to this object of devotion and love [17]. As such, individuals continue expressing their passion and commitment to the objects of affection as they change from time to time. Here, intolerance is expressed towards individuals who fail to adhere or those who tend to criticise the policies and actions that could be considered acceptable for the blind patriots.

The unwavering support for one's nation without tolerance for criticism, as expressed in blind patriotism, has often been associated with political disengagement, nationalism, and selective exposure to information, an aspect related to lower civic participation. Blind patriots have often been defined as individuals who fail to ask difficult questions regarding national leadership, thus increasing the tendency to show loyalty and support the status quo despite the loops and limitations within the institutions[18].

Constructive patriotism covers more relaxed and acceptable components of devotion and love for one's country. It addresses the bond between a person and their country as seen by a more open-minded identification, encouragement of constructive criticism, and a desire to bring about positive change in society. Constructive patriotism involves the love for one's country, as shown in the ability of citizens to question and criticize existing policies and actions [18.] This aims to improve current policies and frameworks while seeking to bring about positive changes within nations.

In the long run, constructive patriots reject actions that are considered contrary to the country's interests, thus participating in tasks associated with constructing a positive identity for their groups or nations. A good patriot will likely resist morally repugnant behaviour that might contradict a nation's fundamental principles and be detrimental to the long-term interests of the country. Within modern communities, citizens are moving towards global citizenship based on an increasing need and focus on democracy. Such individuals observe and acknowledge the goodness of the entire humankind.

The patriotism language has been used over the years, showing an individual's or group's love for one's county. It has been used to invoke feelings of love for institutions and countries even as leaders have sought to emphasize common liberty and love for one's republic. Other philosophers feel this definition is too thin to handle all the critical aspects of patriotism. Stephen Nathanson defined patriotism to cover parts of special affection for one's country, a sense of personal identification with the government, and a particular concern for its well-being. The philosopher also emphasized the willingness of citizens to sacrifice their time and resources to promote the country's good[19]. This is characterized by people joining professions such as the military that offer security to the country while promoting its interests to remain peaceful.

The meaning of one's attachment, loyalty, and identity with a political community is defined by an investigation of the term patriotism in its historical and conceptual context. It has long been regarded as a core virtue associated with citizenship as a political idea of the individual. It has, however, remained a highly contested subject resulting in potential conflicts and violence. In a paradox, the willingness of individuals to die or kill for their country has traditionally been considered the most natural form and expression of patriotism. The concept is more complex based on the differences in perspectives among leaders and individuals across the globe regarding what patriotism means[20]. According to the opposing viewpoints, patriotism is seen as a morally wrong position or moral virtue over one's country on the one hand, and a morally right position or moral virtue over one's country on the other.

An attachment to one's country is considered patriotism based on the existence of four elements. These include the presence of a subject and object of patriotism, the nature of the relationship between the subject and object, and the justification for patriotism. These cover the importance, necessity, and urgency of loyalty to one's country. Patriotism encompasses horizontal and vertical aspects. The vertical dimension of patriotism comprises the connection between an individual and their own country, political community, or geographical area. This aspect covers the relationship between the subject and object of patriotism[21]. This dimension revolves around a political community or country's cultural, linguistic, historical, and traditional aspects. On the other hand, the political aspect of patriotism is centred on a sense of emotional attachment to and allegiance to shared ideas and fundamental principles. Pre-political patriotism refers to the bond that exists between a territory and the residents of a certain geographic area based on the existence of common values and guiding principles.

The cultural, social, and psychological ties that exist between a political community and its constituents are intimately related to the horizontal dimension of patriotism. A sense of cohesion and solidarity among members is fostered by the presence of a shared political identity[22]. This conforms to Robert Audi's definition of patriotism, which includes traits of character, feelings, and positions pertaining to the loyalty a person shows to their nation.

Nature of Patriotism

Two different conceptions of patriotism exist, covering both the vertical and horizontal aspects of patriotism. Extreme notions of patriotism at the vertical level cover elements of unconditional loyalty to one's county as represented by the slogan "my country: right or wrong" [23]. The defence of patriotism among subjects is absolute; hence the object of patriotism receives unconditional support. Consequently, this is characterized by a total attachment to one's country as shown in love attached to it and giving priority to one's compatriots.

Moderate conceptions of patriotism are subject to procedural and object-related limitations. These are aimed at giving the concepts of patriotism a sufficient degree of legitimacy necessary to limit the potential adverse effects.

Patriotism has been associated with the challenge of partiality. The complete version of patriotism covers instances in which an individual's love for compatriots precedes other groups and individuals. This is done despite the policies to cultivate and support one's country. The relative version of patriotism is characterised by the ability of individuals to favour compatriots and members of a particular political community based on specific conditions and circumstances [24]. This is manifested in various forms, including the need for an individual to possess special obligations for their compatriots. Some of these obligations cover elements such as voting, offering services in the country's justice system, keeping a watchful eye, and protesting unethical activities by the government.

The problem of partiality in patriotism affects the ability of individuals to be attached to other fellow citizens versus the commitment to equal respect for all other individuals outside one's nation or country.

History of Patriotism

Patriotism owes its origin to an estimated 2,000 years before the rise and popularisation of nationalism. It is perceived to have originated in the Roman and Greek empires, where people owed loyalty to the *Patria* based on the ongoing political conception of the republic. In the past, patriotism owed its existence to the likelihood of people showing love of the laws and common liberty. Consequently, patriots were thought to search for the common good in societies and thus behaved justly towards their country.

It is believed that the emergence of Christianity resulted in the spread of giving Caesar what belonged to Caesar and God what was his. In a sense, this resulted in divided loyalties among Christians for the government on the one hand and divinity on the other hand [25]. The move towards Christianity brought confusion as people were left to determine the extent of their loyalty to their God and the governing authorities.

In the seventeenth century, patriotism seemed like a forgotten concept, especially in Europe, where princes were rulers over the people who were now considered subjects. Dominion over subjects resulted in forced obedience as subjects were under the rule of the leaders. As such, they were unlikely to possess any sense of belongingness and the need to show allegiance to their nations over other sovereignties and political affiliations[26]. By 1726, patriotism was mentioned as defined to mean the degree of public-spiritedness, which was a characteristic of citizens and not subjects.

Patriotism was now linked to the rise of sovereignty as nations sought to gain independence from each other. The rise of liberty is attributed to the increasing focus and recognition of men's rights, resulting in the formation of governments beginning with America and then France. In this era, patriotism arose from the increased enlightenment of people and the increasing focus on exercising their rights.

Arguments against Patriotism

Patriotism has received praise and criticism in equal measure. While proponents of the concept show the extent to which individuals express love for their nations, the opponents cite the extent to which the expression of such love could impact others considered outsiders to the specified country. One famous critic of patriotism is Tolstoy, the Russian writer and thinker, who starts by defining the term as the preference of one's country over others. The superiority and preference associated with the definition span through nations with each people preferring their countries or nations over others[19]. While this could be a concept that elevates one nation above others, it is simply impossible to rate countries based on their superiority. Here, there would be a need to place countries where they belong relative to the evaluating factors. The idea of a country being superior to others is far-fetched based on countries' unique features and characteristics based on their sizes, climates, political powers, natural beauty, economic productivity, cultural richness, and justice within institutions. It would be impossible for a nation to score ideally based on these features; hence, it is impossible to rate a country as superior based on the presenting features.

While opposition exists to the feeling of superiority expressed in the concept of patriotism, nations have often shown themselves superior to others. The Jewish nation has often defined itself as the chosen people. The Americas on the other hand refer to themselves as the greatest nation on earth. Germans also expressed their sense of superiority based on their racial advantages with the French citing their linguistic and cultural superiority[27]. With the preceding examples of ethnocentric attitudes and behaviours, it would be complex to pinpoint the capabilities of nations and countries relative to one another as one group will prefer and favour their nations over others. People who have failed to hold their nations in high esteem compared to others have often been met with hostility from patriots who feel that their governments should be held with esteem and preference over others despite the prevailing circumstances and capabilities. This has been taken up by political leaders who more often than not use these ideologies to flatter citizens and thus gain acceptance and rewards by affirming to the people that their countries are superior to others. Aspects of familiarity also push citizens towards believing in their nations over others. Societies are often measured based on their capabilities, resources, and criteria.

Nationalism

Nation

To understand nationalism, the concept of a nation crops up. According to the Oxford English Dictionary, a nation is "a large body of people united by common descent, culture, history or language, inhabiting a particular country or territory. Additionally, such people should be conscious of their unity to seek or possess a government peculiarity. An objective definition covers aspects of language, religion, customs, and territory[28]. On the other hand, the subjective elements cover components of people's attitudes, sentiments, and perceptions that make them closer to each other than those who do not share the same values and belief systems.

According to Brubaker, nationhood is a term that has been used over the years to change how people see themselves, mobilize individuals towards expressing loyalty to an institution, government, or leaders, and support an identified group of people to kindle energies and articulate their demands [30].

The concept of national identity is associated with the collective feeling of belongingness to a nation. It refers to the availability or shared interests and qualities that separate individuals or groups from others. From this definition, a country is considered a concept that covers the consciousness that constitutes a group, as well as political, historical, territorial, and cultural characteristics.

Smith describes a nation as a group of people who live together and share a historical location, historical memories, shared mythology, a common culture, and legal obligations and rights for all of its citizens.[31]. Here, an emphasis is made on the peculiarity associated with belonging or having claims to an identified piece of land. Focus on the land is based on the fact that it is not just an ordinary piece of land. Instead, it is the land that turns a society of the same kind into a nation or, in other words, a native country. Consequently, a nation can be defined by extension as a piece of land with clearly marked and identified borders with individuals located in addition to obeying the established unitary administration. Here, reference is made to the community, a group of people brought together by a psychological structure revealed through a shared cultural expression and common language.

Differences between a Nation and a State

The term nation is differentiated from the state because a state refers to an association of people characterised by formal government institutions, including awareness and adherence to laws, permanent territorial boundaries, and sovereignty in terms of political decisions and perspectives. The critical components for state formation revolve around population, government, territory, and sovereignty[32]. The absence of one of the elements stated above defeats the definition of the state and calls for the inclusion of all the aforementioned components for a geographic location to be termed a state. A nation, on the other hand, comprises a series of elements that supports the formation of a nation. These include the existence of a common territory, common race, religion, language, history, culture, and political aspirations. This calls for commonality in individuals' belief systems, actions, and norms within a specified geographic region.

While the connection of states covers the existence of a political organisation, actions, and decisions, nations cover components of social, cultural, psychological, and political unity. The state exists to fulfil its people's welfare and security needs while a nation exists as a united unit of the population characterized by emotional, psychological, and spiritual bonds. Rarely does a nation cater to the physical needs of its citizens. Another crucial differentiating factor lies with the existence of a defined territory[33]. A state must have a fixed physical element, characterized by a territorial entry while this is not necessary for a nation. A nation can therefore exist or survive without the existence of a fixed territory. One's love for a common motherland can act as a source of unity. An example is the existence of a Jewish nation before 1948 without the presence of a fixed and marked physical territory [34]. Following this period, the nation secured a definite and defined settlement establishing the state of Israel.

Sovereignty is essential for a state and not a nation. For a given territory to be considered a state, it should have the capacity to govern itself by creating policies, laws, and frameworks that inform decision-making, action, and processes within the defined physical location. In the absence of sovereignty, a state loses its existence[35]. In contrast, it is not a must for a nation to possess independence. The essential requirement as regards nations revolves around solid bonds of emotional unity among people developing due to everyday social and cultural elements.

Nations can be more comprehensive than states as individuals across defined boundaries could possess similar cultures, descent and common language, among other defining characteristics. An example is the French nation that extends beyond Belgium, Italy, and Switzerland, yet the same racial identity binds all the inhabitants within these regions. Serbian people live all over the Balkan; however, they are often called Montenegrians, Bosnians even Croatians or Macedonians.

Other critical characteristics of a nation include increased stability based on a standard tie that binds people together instead of artificially created factors such as political organisations. For example, Germany and Japan lost their sovereignty status at the close of the Second World War and were left under the control of outside powers[36]. These two countries ceased to exist as states. However, they continued to exist as nations, eventually becoming sovereign independent states. Moreover, states are created yet nations emerge as a result of evolution. Physical elements contribute significantly to the creation of states. For example, following the end of World War II, Germany was divided into two self-governing states, East and West Germany. Yet the whole territory remains as a nation based on the existence of a common area of descent, history, language, and ways of life. In a sense, a nation develops through various changes without active efforts towards its creation. This was not the case when we are talking about the Kingdom of Serbs Croats and Slovenians for example. After WW2, they all became Yugoslav, and once ex-Yugoslavia collapsed in 1992, Croatia and Slovenia became independent while Serbia was split into Serbia, Montenegro, Bosnia and Hercegovina, North Macedonia, and Kosovo. An extremely confusing process in which Serbs completely lost their sense of identity due to the process of depersonalisation during the fifty years of communist dictatorship. On the other hand, East Germans didn't lose their sense of national identity and they kept united.

States apply force to preserve their unity and integrity, whereas a nation is bound by the existence of strong historical and cultural links. A nation is backed by the existence of moral, spiritual, and emotional powers characterised by the sense of unity among people considered to belong to the same nation. A nation conducts activities around appeals, persuasion, and boycotts, whereas a state order coerces and punishes. In modern society, most states comprise multiple nations. My personal view is very simple. Nations are born very quickly, but they also die even quicker. The human psychological need to belong is human's biggest weakness and causes more harm than good to humans.

Ethnic Community

Ethnicity is understood as an individual's inherited status based on the place of residence. It refers to the state of belonging to a subgroup or population characterised by identifiable physical and social attributes. Ethnicity refers to the ethnic identity of a person ascertained by descent-based characteristics connoting the traits connected to one's descent. Those characteristics have been acquired as a result of cultural or historical inheritance. People of the same ethnic descent consider themselves distinct from others based on social, ancestral, and national heritage[37]. People belonging to the same ethnic community share a common language, history, traditions, dialect, culture, physical appearance, and other similar factors such as geographical affiliation to particular places, foods, beliefs, and dressing style, among other differentiating characteristics. The Indian population is estimated at around 1.2 billion people belonging to different ethnic communities such as Bengali, Punjabi, Rajasthani, and Marathi, among other ethnic categories.

Ethnicity denotes an individual's ethnic identity based on descent attributes while nations bring together individuals based on membership in nations. While the ethnicity of an individual can be based on factors such as dialects, dressing styles, race, and physical characteristics, the nationality of individuals is based on one's country of origin[38]. Another crucial differentiating factor lies in ethnicity being associated with heritage and ancestry while nationality is conferred on an individual based on their country of origin.

Definition of Nationalism

Loyalty and dedication to a nation are the definitions of nationalism. It is centred on the idea of national consciousness, in which people elevate one nation above all others while prioritising the promotion of that nation's culture and interests over those of other nations.

Another definition of nationalism describes it as an ideology practised by people who think their country is better than all others. The components of a nation's superiority are built on shared social and cultural values, language, religion, and ethnicity.

Other meanings of the term have been expressed as follows:

❖ The process of formation or growth of nations
❖ Sense of belongingness to a nation
❖ Language and symbols that normally represent a nation
❖ Social and political movements that represent a nation
❖ Doctrines or ideologies of a nation cover the general and particular aspects of processes and operations.

Nationalism is used to describe the attitude of citizens of a nation in a bid to care for their national identity. It also covers the actions taken by members as they seek to achieve self-determination. The term has often been used to define an ideology held by people who believe that their nations are superior to all others[39]. This is based on the shared ethnicity of people within national boundaries. In other contexts, nationalism is based on shared religion, culture, social values, and religious beliefs. It is exhibited in individuals based on shared symbols, mythology, and common history.

Nationalism is based on the premise that individuals are loyal and devoted to their nation-state with a passion that surpasses other individuals and group interests. Nationalism has been closely linked to the increasing desire for power among leaders of nations. Every nationalist strives to secure more power and prestige for their nation.

Ideology of Nationalism

Ideologies refer to contested concepts with propagators using images and symbols to convince people to believe and act in a certain way. Nationalism is regarded as a political philosophy that makes use of the notion of a nation to advance political objectives[40]. The term ideology has been used differently by different scholars and theorists. According to Marx and Engels, it has been considered a set of ideas that induce false consciousness among workers under capitalism.

As an ideology, nationalism entails developing a world view centred on a collection of consistent beliefs and principles that explain the acts and conduct of a social group today and forecast their future course and behaviour. Nationalism lacks a direct theory of human nature based on the presumption that a nation is a natural unit that binds individuals and communities together, putting their welfare first. The idea prioritises national loyalty over all other types of political and social loyalty[41]. Even if someone may be devoted to their morals and religion, nationalism holds that in the event of a conflict between the two philosophies, allegiance to the country must take precedence. Thus, nationalism makes a nation the focus of political allegiance, insisting on its proper organisation based on political activity. Thus, a nation comprised of individuals and communities can claim property, lives, and other sacrifices among its members to ensure the collective survival of those within its borders.

Another everyday use of the term relates to classifying concepts into left and right ideologies common in day-to-day politics, such as socialism, communism, conservatism, and liberalism. From the two categories above, nationalism is considered a third type of ideology that revolves around creating and maintaining political units, enabling proponents to pursue other ideologies in relation to the left and right policy prescriptions.

Core Structure of Nationalism

Michael Freeden discussed five elements of nationalism as follows:

1. Prioritisation of a particular group as a foundational framework for humans and their practices. Here, citizens of specific sovereignty or nation are considered key in all processes and policies established to guide and protect them. Categorising individuals into a country is not based on any particular form; instead, the process could follow imagined or constructed views of homogeneity or pluralistic perspective of individuals and classes within a nation[42]. Here, the concepts of liberal and illiberal nationalism arise with proponents supporting a pluralistic view of classification in which all the other aspects that different individuals within a nation are absorbed. Consequently, this results in the classification of nationalists into functional, religious, and regional/global communities. Functional communities comprise the classification and categorisation of individuals based on functional rather than territorial groups. Examples include bringing people across various classes, cultures, religious classes, and political groups to work together based on their belongingness to an identified geographical boundary. Religious communities cover the establishment of loyalties based on shared religious beliefs and practices.

2. Investments in capital, material, and human resources are made to enhance the value of a nation through the adoption of customized policies addressing the specific needs of individuals and people within the nation. Here, a positive polarisation is assigned to

specific countries, allowing leaders to practice specific claims regarding members' conduct and overall performance.

3. Another crucial consideration for nationalism lies in the ability and responsibility of leaders to create political institutions to govern the citizens and prioritize their needs over those that fall outside the nation.

4. Elements of space and time are considered crucial for determining the social identity of individuals. This could be based on their place of origin, common language, culture, and religious beliefs, among others.

5. A nation is characterised by a sense of belongingness in which members expresses themselves through sentimental elements and expression of emotions. Those belonging to the same nation are likely to team up against outsiders. Nationalism revolves around land and territories specifically marked. Nationalists claim the centrality of specific tracts of land to them, their people, and their collective history, cultures, and traditions[43]. Emotional attachment to land covers elements of ownership, appropriation, and the inclusion of one's nation on the one hand and exclusion of others on the other hand.

Nationalism as an ideology, therefore, places a nation as the major centre of concern with proponents seeking to promote its well-being over and above those of others. The main goals of such ideologies cover aspects of national autonomy, unity, and identity. National sovereignty covers the elements in which nations seek to be independent of others. They aim at gaining and maintaining the right to self-government and self-determination[44]. Here, countries are granted the right to govern themselves and control specific territories and people living within the marked boundaries.

According to nationalism, the country and the state should complement one another. This means that the idea advances a country's interests in upholding its sovereignty. Every country ought to be self-governing, free from outside intervention, and exercising self-determination. Therefore, the idea advocates for forging and preserving a unified national identity based on shared ethnicity, language, geography, religion, traditions, and beliefs in a common past. Such decisions and activities are intended to enhance solidarity and national unity. Nationalism has been associated with an increased desire among people, particularly the ruling elite class, to protect and advance a country's historic culture.

Nationalism also aims at creating a unique culture among people identified and classified as belonging to the same nation. Here, individuals are expected to have a common culture, an understanding of the aspects, and the same aspirations for the future of a nation. Such interests are likely to bind people within a nation together and enable them to fight for the nation's interests collectively[45]. While national identity has been linked to elements and acts of aggression and persecution when taken in its extreme forms, it has also been considered positive, built around democratic political values, and shared experiences across communities to maintain successful modern political order among nations. Additionally, national identity has contributed to physical security while inspiring good governance, facilitating economic development in modern nations, and fostering higher levels of trust among citizens.

The phrase has also been used to refer to an intellectual movement that works to establish and uphold the autonomy, unity, and sense of self of a demographic group whose members view themselves as making up a nation, either real or imagined

Types of Nationalism

Ethnic Nationalism

Ethnic nationalism identifies a close connection between national members linked together by race, language, and cultural attributes persisting for centuries among people. An individual is considered a member of a nation based on birth and bloodline, genetics, and identity that individuals cannot forfeit for becoming a citizen of another nation or acquired by filing an application to be considered as part of another nation. An example is an application made by ethnic Germans, currently considered Russians, to rejoin their nation and German culture based on their origins and descent characteristics.

Ethnic nationalism is characterised by the demand for nationhood among people with common ancestry or descent. The Germans practised an example of this kind of nationalism between the nineteenth and twentieth centuries. It is characterised by cultural, linguistic, and religious nationalism elements where individuals are categorised based on their ethnic standing, religious beliefs, and common language[46]. With this in mind, nationalism has been cited as a factor that divided people across religious beliefs, language, and even within families. Within this calcification lies linguistic nationalism characterised by the division of people across linguistic lines. This is exemplified by the call for the cessation of Bangladesh from Pakistan in 1971 based on the choice of language by the Pakistani nation.

Aspects of cultural nationalism cover the elements of ethnicity together with culture [47]. This allows individuals to acquire nationalism through other means than ethnic background. Its proponents hold that an individual can be considered part of a nation through circumstances such as marriage or residence.

Civic nationalism, on the other hand, covers aspects of common historical ties between people in the nation. These ties can easily be extruded to others through citizenship, loyalties, and obligations linked to acquiring a nation's citizenship[48]. Here, limitations do not exist regarding individuals who can be considered part of a nation. However, it is difficult to attain this form of nationalism based on restrictions and required thresholds for individuals to be considered part of modern nations. For one to be considered, they have to fulfil the established guidelines and frameworks that could prevent individuals from becoming part of a nation. Existing members of a nation may establish objections regarding the large-scale addition of people to the nation through acquired citizenship.

The sense of belongingness to a nation arises from the consent and active participation of citizens as free members of a democratic political community. Membership in civic nations can be obtained through immigration and renunciation of other allegiances and birth. This calls for the creation of liberal democratic institutions and the design of a constitution to consider the interest of all citizens. Representative democracy ensures that the rights of all citizens are honoured. This form of nationalism is closely linked to modern society, where an individual's descent, ethnicity, religion, and other defining components do not take centre stage[49]. The United States of America and France have long been considered nations that depict civic nationalism. Others have evolved into this concept based on open immigration and mobility policies allowing people from across all regions of the world to enter and settle in these countries for personal and communal benefits. These include German and Indian evolving from ethnic and anti-colonial nationalism, respectively.

In civic nationalism, ethnicity is considered inferior to shared citizenship of people, the existence of common institutions, values, and respect for constitutional rights and obligations of individuals within national boundaries. Here, the patriotism of individuals is similar even though one could be born and bred in the nation with the other acquiring citizenship through aspects such as naturalisation, birth, and immigration to the nations of choice. Here, patriotic feelings are linked to constitutional elements over allegiance to the political aspects of a nation as founded on descent-related factors. As stated earlier, the United States of America is the epitome of civic nationalism based on the existence of diverse ethnicities brought together by their allegiance and respect for the country's constitution[50]. Other elements that unite the United States citizens include the values and practices developed over time as people moved in with diverse cultures calling for adopting acceptable and ethical practices to support their peaceful coexistence.

Civic nationalism acknowledges the interactions between the components of belongingness and citizenship and their related affiliations as necessary for forming nations. Here, citizens neglect components of descent that could bring them together, such as religion, ethnicity, and language. Instead, they focus on the sense of mutual commitment among citizens towards upholding shared ideals, rules, and values. Citizens accept the existence of diversities with the increasing need for mutual understanding and coexistence.

This goes in line with the thoughts of German philosopher Theodor Adorno. He proposed that an emancipated society is characterized by the realisation of universality, enabling people with diverse characteristics to reconcile their differences[51]. He emphasised the need for the existence of a society where people could be allowed to be different without fear and anxiety of being picked on. This modern concept of nationalism is attributed to the current societies characterised by the existence of inclusive, multi-ethnic societies with multiple religious beliefs as opposed to the need for similar cultural and historic features characterizing individuals of a specified nationality.

Civic nationalism appreciates those elements such as ethnicity, linguistics, and cultures that form the basis of a nation, yet those should be allowed to evolve based on the presenting circumstances. Such evolutions and changes result in the formation of civilised, respectful, equal, and welcoming societies that consider the unique features of individuals while protecting their rights without partiality and favouritism. Actions and decisions in civic nations are guided by the existence of a network of institutions mandated to check and provide a balance on the power of the rulers and governments while upholding democracy for the good of all citizens. Other formal mechanisms to ensure the peaceful coexistence of citizens within nations include the existence and acceptance of the rule of law, the court system, and parliamentary accountability to provide checks and balances preventing government overreach[52]. Additionally, the opposition is appreciated as an intrinsic part of the governance structure instead of treating such actions as treason as common in other forms of nationalism.

Equal access among citizens to citizenship, education, and community activities is upheld among ethnic nationalities. Establishing policies in such nations considers the interest of all people, including minority groups. National symbols seek to unite rather than divide people while legal structure aims at promoting and upholding the mandates of such institutions. A free economy is crucial in allowing citizens to participate fully and conduct their affairs without undue influence and pressure.

Religious Nationalism

This is considered a subset of ethnic nationalism—the concept privileges nationalism as a foundation for nationhood. In India, there was an increased push among Muslims to preserve Pakistan as a nation for Indian Muslims[53]. This proposition, however, received opposition based on the challenge that Islam could not be confined within the territorial boundaries of nations.

Another crucial component of nationalism is classified as territorial nationalism. This concept defines the nationhood of people based on their defined territories. New Zealand, for example, exhibits territorial nationalism based on its isolation from the rest of the world and the existence of a shared history among its people[54]. This has also been exhibited in the Gambia based on its isolation from the rest of the world.

Liberal Nationalism

According to liberal nationalists, humankind is divided into nations characterized by the existence of the same territorial boundaries. Each country should be independent and have its own political structures. Human rights are viewed as universal and similar in these places.

Liberal nationalism is common among international pacifist and idealist elements with liberalism. As such, the concepts result in the existence of worlds of sovereign nations in which respect for national rights and cooperation among international institutions is held in high esteem[55]. Such nationalism involves the respect for minority rights, whether classified in the form of linguistics, ethnic or religious beliefs. This form of nationalism was common among socialists and liberals in the nineteenth century. Following the First World War, it was resurrected following the establishment of the League of Nations, founded on the principles of collective security among nations and national self-determination. An example of such an embodiment is the formation of the United Nations as a body that looks into the rights of individuals and nations despite their diverse cultures, political views, economic positions, and other classified characteristics. Such international bodies were established to regulate human rights while creating free trade and promoting cooperation and collaboration in international trade.

Liberal economists underestimated the challenges associated with the identification of natural national units based on aspects of geography, population, and economic viability. They disregarded the potential of nationalism to cause harm while focusing on the positive aspects of such collaborations and cooperation between diverse nations with different perspectives and views[56]. Despite the initial concerns and challenges, liberal nationalism remains a vital element in many modern nationalistic movements.

Reactionary Nationalism

The liberal nationalist revolutions of 1848 failed to achieve objectives for people and communities across various European territories. These movements were becoming more and more linked to reactionary and conservative forces that were concerned with establishing and defending countries and their institutions against elements of socialism and revolution. Thus, nationalism evolved into a strategy for stifling or suppressing some citizens' national identities in order to promote national unity as a whole[57]. The multinational Austro-Hungarian and Russian empires, which were battling rising nationalism while attempting to assert imperialism, nationalism, and unity against the escalating aspirations for more autonomy and independence from the submissive states, were exemplified by these global movements.

The idea of reactionary nationalism emerged in Europe around the 1870s, following the founding of the Third French Republic and the union of Germany, and it quickly spread throughout the continent. This concept was closely linked to organic identity expressed in the forms of religion, traditional hierarchies, culture, customs, and social order. This type of nationalism transcended national lines and was marked by elements of imperialism, racism, and claims of states' right to rule over less-developed nations through the use of political and military competition with other nations. Such elements of nationalism instilled ideological alternatives in the minds of enfranchised masses[58]. At the end of the twentieth century, reactionary nationalism had been linked with conservatism resulting in increased efforts by socialists and radicals to distance themselves from the nationalism of their opponents in most western democracies. This kind of nationalism was characterized by a focus on aspects of patriotism and its unique nature yet it remained indifferent to the events outside the nation as long as such did not interfere with its affairs.

Radical Nationalism

Radical nationalism emerged after the First World War even though the concept could be traced back to the French revolutionaries. The concept is connected to the desire of individuals or nations to change the domestic or international order in favour of one's nation. It takes either the aspect of the rightist form of politics on one hand or the mainstay of anti-colonialism on the other. The radical right form of nationalism despised the old order, outdated institutions, and the less privileged classes, which had been condemned as having betrayed the nation. These changes revolved around social, political, and economic reforms to renew the nation[59]. Such strategies targeted offering the working classes alternatives to concepts such as the internationalisation of socialism and communism following the Russian revolution. This concept of nationalism is aimed at overthrowing an existing system or state without necessarily changing the cultural, territorial, and linguistic characteristics.

Defeat in wars across Germany and Turkey resulted in this kind of nationalism across these regions. The concept was also felt across Italy and France as a result of wars within and without such nations. Radical nationalism was characterised by intolerance for minorities that had been treated as outsiders to the nation. In its extreme forms, radical nationalism sets the stage for the superiority of other nations and leads to war justification against others considered enemies. During WW2, Croatians had the same view on Serbs, Jews, and gipsies, resulting in the holocaust of primary Serbs but also Jews and Gypsies in the Independent State of Croatia. With this in mind, this kind of nationalism can easily be regarded as fascism[60].

On the other hand, the concept can take an opposite path related to the anti-colonial struggle against imperial or reactionary radical nationalism. The focus on independence from the current political systems, which are perceived as oppressive by the citizens of a nation, can be one example of radical nationalism in this context. As a result, it supports the idea of national independence and the right of nations to self-determination. The ending of the European empires following the Second World War is attributed to this kind of nationalism.

A historical analysis of radical nationalism reveals a close relationship between social components connected to indigenous societies' community values and the subsequent overthrow of the colonial ruling class. Following independence, radical nationalism manifested itself as opposition to western economic, political, and cultural hegemony, which led to the nationalisation of the assets of multinational firms in developing nations.

Diaspora Nationalism

A diaspora refers to a migrant community crossing borders from its original homeland while maintaining its ethnic group consciousness and peculiar institutions over time. It covers an ancient social formation that comprises people living out of their ancestral homeland while retaining their loyalties towards their ethnic identities and populations and their homeland[61]. The Jews and Assyrians have historically been considered diaspora based on their unique history and evolution stories. Other groups such as the Palestinians, Armenians, and Chinese have recently settled outside their natal territories while maintaining solid collective identities. They have been categorised as individuals exhibiting diaspora nationalism.

This kind of nationalism is characterised by the tendency for people living in foreign countries to advocate, finance, and arm nationalistic movements in their home countries. This is attributed to the nostalgia associated with the need for an ideal territory in the countries they have left. More often than not, proponents of diaspora nationalism preserve their homeland's ideas, beliefs, and practices even after they have been abandoned by people who remained in such places. The love and passion for one's nation are characterised by financial transfers and remittances to aid those left in the homeland. The actions of the diaspora are often fuelled by radical and political agendas in their home countries. An example of diaspora nationalism lies with the sustainability of Jewish nationhood even though the Jews were spread all around the globe[62]. This came to an end in 1948 following the formation of Israel as a Jewish nation.

Polyethnic Nationalism

Polyethnicity has been considered a crucial component in the social development of social status in the contemporary world. The aspects cover the combination of the existence of indigenous people, immigration conquest, and land divisions resulting from wars over the evolution of the two world's history[63]. Migration is a crucial element of polyethnicity attributed to having created nations based on its influence on the internal development of countries by producing and applying the cultural and social capital of an identified population group.

The History of Nationalism

Sense of national differences and identification with kings, princes, languages, and cultures was common before the period of the European renaissance. Such actions were based on universalist claims and loyalty to the concept of Christendom as characterised by the pope and the Holy

Roman Empire in the face of threats from the Muslim world. Following the European renaissance, a sense of national identity was created. Concepts of shared language, adoption of explicit national cultures, and national religion were common occurrences strengthening the sense of national differences. Consequently, aspects of national identity and support for strong centralised states were created with an increasing ability to create national loyalty among population groups.

Most nationalism theories assume that the concept was first applied in the eighteenth century in Europe. Before the nineteenth century, it is believed that people had no idea of nationalism but had religious, regional, and local loyalties. European states initially carried out national unity and identity since they were crucial in modernizing society and the economy[64]. States in Europe were dynastic, governed by royal houses. In situations where loyalties beyond a region were owed to the ruling house and the king, dynastic states could obtain territory through royal marriages and lose them through inheritance, an idea that seems absurd today.

The agricultural and industrial revolutions of the eighteenth and nineteenth centuries led to the dissolution of many allegiances without their replacement by new ones. Thus, nations would develop and take their place. The emergence of nationalism was greatly influenced by the French, American, and Napoleonic wars. Before the emergence of such conflicts, individuals expressed their loyalty toward others in leadership positions, such as the monarchs. Following the French wars, ancient French regimes were overthrown, resulting in an increased stimulation and focus on the aspects of nationalism based on standard practices and identities among individuals[65]. As a result of wars, the highest form of political loyalty to the monarch shifted to an increased focus on the nation resulting in the generally accepted principle that the nation was a natural social organisation.

The conquests of Napoleon Bonaparte and the French revolution led to nationalist movements in Europe. As Napoleon extended the central government of France into all the countries he had conquered in the European region, the French started defining themselves as to what they were and were not. Military victories from such conquests brought the French people together, creating a shared sense of history and identity, thus strengthening a sense of nationalism in the region[66]. In a paradox, as the French gained victory over its enemies, the enemies felt that national determination was the way to go. They united against the French rulers, creating a sense of nationalism amongst themselves.

As conquests continued, the enemies organised themselves into nations to fight against such unfair treatment by the superpowers. Napoleon ended up bringing changes to the traditional forms of leadership characterized by regimes led by kings, queens, and subjects to create nations made up of citizens and parliaments from which laws could be drawn to protect a nation's and citizens' rights against those of others.

Other critical considerations in this movement were the growth of large cities due to migration from the land to the cities. The increase in literacy and formal education resulted in the branding of university students among the early nationalists of all times.

Some movements, such as the Greek Revolution of 1821–1829, were directed against some large empires. On the contrary, others tried to unite a divided territory. These movements enhanced national culture and identity. Scholars believe that the concept of nationalism was firmly established in the nineteenth century[67]. In the history of nationalism, the French Revolution in 1789 is viewed as a significant beginning point for France and its influence on European, Italian, and German intellectuals.

In the mid-eighteenth century, the British government, intellectuals, and writers actively promoted the rise of widespread patriotic nationalism. Consequently, nationalists started constructing narratives, myths, anthems, flags, and national symbols, which became widely accepted. Towards the end of the nineteenth, the concept of nationalism started to spread to other continents, such as Asia. As a result, nationalists in India began to agitate to end British rule. In Europe, the world war also led to the development of new nation-states, which was encouraged by America, and refused the legality of the previous multi-ethnic empires.

Nationalism in the 20th Century

Towards the end of the nineteenth century, the idea of nationalism started to spread in Asia. Nationalism in India began to call for the end of British rule. Mahatma Gandhi is usually linked to the twentieth-century nationalist movement in India although other leaders were involved. Nationalism in China, on the other hand, led to the revolution of 1911. The creation of new states in Europe resulted from World War I. This resulted from the United States denying the legitimacy of the previous multi-ethnic empires.

Twentieth-century nationalism is considered an era of total warfare, strengthening nationalism simultaneously. During this time, the viability and value of nations as political units were questioned. Its connection to human affairs was also challenged due to the increasing warfare between nations resulting in untold ruin, deaths, and destruction of property. The twentieth-century wars were considered too destructive as they were characterised by loss of lives and property, leading to an increasing question of the aspects of nationalism and whether it was an enabling factor for the continued bloodshed[68]. As a result of the wars, opponents of the concept of nationalism felt that those in favour of organised groups needed to have considered the needs of other populations without merely focusing on their own.

Following the end of the Second World War, there was an increased focus on liberation movements boosting the nature of struggles towards fascist nationalism. Consequently, nationalism was considered a dangerous and destructive force due to increased violence and intolerance of diverse political agendas and perspectives.

Militant nationalism as an ideology was discredited during World War II but did not change Europe's division into nation-states. Away from Europe, World War II led to the formation of new nation-states through the independence of African and Asian countries from colonial kingdoms. An example is the decolonisation that started in the 1950s in Africa. The latter half of the twentieth century has led to some trends that weakened nationalism and the nation-state.

The end of Cold War and the collapse of the Soviet Union occurred at a time when globalisation was becoming a driving force among communities. At this point, there was an increased focus on establishing and strengthening international institutions to cover the weaknesses associated with national politics and actions. The USSR and Yugoslavia were among the countries that were consistently suppressed, which led to the collapse of communism and the rise of nationalism in those countries[69]. Due to this, battles broke out in Yugoslavia, resulting in extensive destruction and fatalities.

Nationalism in the 21st Century

The concept of nationalism now influences global politics. A unique set of challenges have arisen due to changes in the ethnic/racial composition of people in countries resulting from migration and diaspora. These have created social, economic, and cultural networks that bind people across continents and internationally. Globalisation and regional integration have seen the adoption of policies across governments to revise the nation-building agenda[70]. While some nationalist states support globalisation, others see it as a potential threat to the nation-state's legitimacy and authority. Substate nationalists are looking out for support and loyalty from the people. Consequently, nationalists are reconsidering the meaning of nationalist concepts such as autonomy, independence, sovereignty, and self-determination in an interconnected world.

In the twenty-first century, nationalism is considered a component intimately linked to society's interests. It is considered a factor that brings together the aspects of the development of industrialisation and modern statehood. This is attributed to the massive developments in the technological and social aspects of societies resulting in scientific inquiry, increased rationality, and consequent development of centralized states accompanied by social reforms.

Political uses of nationalist ideologies are applied differently by different individuals and communities. For conservatives, nationalist ideologies are used to support the creation of social cohesion and order in societies. Here, the opponents hold that all people within a nation have a place and a role to play. As such, the organic nature of a nation must be protected as a natural social unit. This concept was, however, missed in the late nineteenth century by the British in encouraging political support for themselves as well as support for overseas expansion.

Liberals, on the other hand, hold that nationalism is closely linked to the freedom of individuals and nations. Here, nationalism is considered a crucial means through which the interests of people required for the functionality of the society are balanced in regard to the individualism common in the free-market economy. They propose that national self-determination in combination with free trade is the critical element required to attain world peace[71]. Social democrats, on the other hand, support the liberals' view stressing the importance of a nation over individual needs.

Marxists consider nationalism to be an ideological tool that has developed due to industrialisation.

Nations now face new challenges on the social and economic front. The need for financial stability has seen the globalisation of businesses with countries accepting foreign investors to boost the country's economy and achieve stability. Such a move has brought about increased interconnectedness between cultures and political interdependence. Consequently, nations have witnessed their sovereign powers being eroded with transformation into states characterised by socio-economic spaces that are beyond national boundaries[72]. Nevertheless, people still identify with nations wherever they are. The influence of collective focus on the nationalist agenda has been eroded by the dispersion of people across the globe in search of better employment, business opportunities, and livelihoods.

In response to the financial crisis of 2011, governments all across the world adopted measures to build, develop, and safeguard their national economies in the context of global markets. This is known as economic nationalism. Economic nationalists oppose globalisation in favour of the stability and safety associated with the protectionism of local industries and operations. To these opponents of foreign deals and businesses, revenue generated from trade should be used to meet nations' economic needs, including national security and the building of military power, instead of focusing on social welfare programs[72]. Economic nationalists often oppose immigration based on the belief that the entry of foreigners reduces employment opportunities available to locals.

Changes in national composition supported the position that nationalism was likely to wear down, leading to its demise in the twenty-first century. One of the popular trans-humanism concepts proposed that nationalism was quickly losing ground. More and more people focused on the source of legitimate power as humankind in general and not individuals within specific national boundaries.

Consequently, the goals of politics revolved around protecting human rights as a whole and not the interests of specific individuals based on their nations of origin. The resulting global empire states unfolding before our eyes are not governed by particular groups and ethnicities. Instead, the empire considers that all individuals within national boundaries have the right to provide feedback and lead others through political affiliations and the decision-making associated with inherent voting rights. There is a movement back to imitate the former Roman Empire, whose leadership was drawn from a multi-ethnic elite group bound together by common interests and culture[73]. Individuals from various professions seek to join forces in driving the interest of nations forward while pursuing shared interests and goals for the benefit of humanity despite their origins and national affiliations.

Key Concepts of Nationalism

The nation-state can be defined as a group of people who have a common identity and live within a nation with well-defined borders and a single dominant authority. The government entity has a big impact on how people live, how the community functions, and how those who reside within its borders identify. It also determines how people speak, the laws they follow, and the holidays they observe. The fundamental concepts of a nation-state revolve around the state as a body of government[74]. This covers the rules, laws, government officials, and titles, as well as the physical boundaries of a state. Therefore, the state revolves around the aspects that make a country run from a political point of view. The nation, on the other hand, refers to the people. A shared belief creates the concept of unity and interconnectedness among people within national boundaries.

This calls for a broader definition of the nation-state to capture the components of a nation and a state. Anthony Smith, a significant contributor to the concepts of nation-state and nationalism, argues that a state can be considered a nation-state only if a single ethnic and cultural group inhabits the boundaries of a state when such boundaries extend to cover the boundaries of the ethnic and cultural position of its inhabitants. The definition, therefore, presumes the existence of one nation in one state. This definition has been considered skewed because only 10% of states across the globe meet its definition concepts. In most states, ethnic minorities are excluded from the majority nation by ethnic and cultural nationalists.

A wider definition of a nation-state covers the concept that a state conjoins the political entity of a state with the cultural entity of a nation. The political legitimacy to rule is obtained from the state aspect of the concept, with the state's sovereignty providing the declarative theory of statehood. Here, the state covers the political and geopolitical aspects, while the nation covers the ethnic and cultural elements of the population groups represented in the entity.

Understanding elements forming a nation-state brings out a more straightforward definition of the concept to cover a territorially bounded sovereign polity. As a result, a state governed in the name of a group of people who identify as a nation might be referred to as a nation-state. The people who live within the designated boundaries and their right to self-determination are the source of the leadership unit's legitimacy. The nation-state combines elements of state sovereignty, which acknowledges a country's right to rule itself and its territories free from outside intervention, with the notion of national sovereignty, which addresses a community's right to self-government[74].

National sovereignty emanates from the moral-philosophical principles of popular sovereignty based on the states to which people belong. This means that the legitimate rule of the state requires the people's consent.

The benefits of the nation-state are attributed to the political sovereignty of nations through which the principles of self-determination were practised and international relations were conducted and measured. On the negative, however, the process of nation-building as regards nation-states resulted in conflicts between diverse ethnic, linguistic, religious, and other cultural groups as each sought to shape the new nations based on their interests and identities.

Positives of Nationalism

It is rare to find people within a country speaking the same language, praying the same way and sharing common ancestry and other crucial features that define a nation. Japan, considered one of the most homogenous nations, has an estimated two million people considered ethnic minorities. Other countries are made up of diverse, unique identities calling for the need for them to establish standard guidelines and qualities that bring them together. Positive nationalism has been practised in Indonesia based on the arrangements and principles guiding the nation as per the guiding frameworks established by the country's founding father, Sukarno, referred to as Pancasila[75]. The concept covers five guiding principles which govern the nation, bringing its people together. To be Indonesian, citizens had to acknowledge and adhere to the principles of the belief in one and only

God, just and civilised humanity, the unity of the country, democratic rule based on fair representation, and the strengths of the country's leadership as well as social justice for the country's citizens[76].

Pancasila is an example of how a belief in shared values and principles can unify a diverse group of individuals. The concept supports social cohesion while contributing significantly to the citizen's pride in their country. It is worth noting that national identities built around characteristics such as ethnicity, language, and culture are likely to exclude individuals who do not meet such criteria. Building national identities around ideas promotes inclusivity and is more accepting. In cognisance of such factors, modem nations have sought to build their national unities and heritages around ideas such as freedom and equality of their citizens. For such nations, liberal principles are enshrined in their laws and constitutions to bind citizens while ensuring adherence to them to achieve national unity and the well-being of nations.

Negatives of Nationalism

Nationalism is considered harmful when it negatively impacts people and their standard ways of life. Narrow and aggressive forms of nationalism will likely place people into groups based on their identifying characteristics. Consequently, people are categorised into groups or considered outsiders even if they exist within those identified as belonging to specified national boundaries[77]. Such definitions and classifications are created to advance the interests of certain groups over others. This phenomenon is called social affiliation.

Extreme nationalism is considered intolerant and illiberal, failing to accept those individuals considered outside the narrow defining characteristics. The mentality that classifies individuals into 'us' versus 'them' based on racial and national superiority could likely result in violent and dangerous ends. Extreme nationalism is characterized by the tendency of individuals and groups to advance a nation's interests above those of others resulting in far-reaching consequences [46]. Such beliefs and actions are considered precipitating factors for world wars. The belief in the superiority of the Aryan community by the Germans resulted in violence and the extermination of individuals who had not been classified as belonging to this group. The manifestation of ethnocentric nationalism fuelled increasing strife between communities, thus resulting in the Second World War[78]. Such convictions sparked the deadliest wars in recorded human history, including horrifying campaigns for identity-based violence like the Holocaust and the systematic murder of Jews and Serbs by the Nazi administration.

Following the end of World War II and the far-reaching consequences and impact on property and lives, the European Union was formed to promote regional security and prosperity of the region far above national. The rising tides of nationalism are, however, causing countries to question such partnerships. There are increasing disagreements as characterised by the recent exit of the United Kingdom from the Union for the country to govern itself away from the influences of the international body. Aspects of identity and exclusive nationalism in other parts of Europe have led to aggressive foreign policies that undermine the global order. By stating that its actions are intended to intervene and help ethnic Russians residing in Ukraine, the Russian government is defending its annexing of Crimea on the basis of its nationalistic beliefs[79]. While Western officials rubbished these claims, there have been strife and developments since 2014, resulting in the ongoing war between the countries.

Ukrainian self-determination was based on a distinct language. It is believed that modern Ukrainian nationalism originated from Kyiv and Eastern Ukraine ruled by the Russian imperial rule and mass movement affecting the western part of the country under Austria-Hungarian law[80]. Following the different influences in the western and eastern parts of the country, further developments of the nations were considered by the eastern side, which was initially ruled by the Russian imperial party, to be a plot aimed at weakening their country and sovereignty.

Three decades of independence have seen Ukraine's efforts at forging a path for itself as a sovereign state and the continued alignment with western institutions such as the EU and NATO. However, cases of internal divisions have affected the nation's effort to achieve these objectives. A more nationalistic Ukrainian population on the western side of the country has been focused on supporting the country's greater integration with Europe while the people of Russian origin in the eastern part of the country are more inclined towards establishing closer ties with their motherland Russia.

Russia possesses deep economic, cultural, and political bonds with Ukraine. In various instances, Ukraine has been cited as the central factor in Russia's identity and vision of itself. The two countries have strong family ties because Kyiv has been considered crucial for the emergence of Russian cities[81]. This city brought Christianity to Russia; thus, Russians point their religious beliefs to this region. According to Laruelle, Russia's actions in Crimea have been aimed at protecting the lives of the Russian diaspora[82]. At the moment, it is believed that approximately eight million Russians live in Ukraine. Following the collapse of the Soviet Union, Russian politicians have been against the independence of Ukraine as this has been considered a threat to Russia's standing as a great power[83]. The nationalistic views regarding Russia's superpower and superiority in the region have been affected by Ukraine's independence affecting Russia's international prestige.

Ongoing wars are attributed to the continuing resistance from the Ukraine government, which believes in their nation's sovereignty and independence from any foreign influence, including Russia. A pre-war poll showed that Ukrainians were willing to take up arms and defend their country against Russian invasion. This is based on the growth of a generation that brings together Ukrainian speakers in the western and Russian-speaking Ukrainians in the eastern part of the country[84]. Consequently, the government has maintained robust democracy over the past three decades. The outbreak of the current war has been cited for having unified Ukrainian citizens from the two regions despite linguistic and religious backgrounds while reinforcing the split between Russian and Ukrainian identities.

Russian President Putin has been vocal in his speech, claiming that Russians and Ukrainians comprised one people based on their common historical origins and should adopt a common political fate today and in the future. This line of thinking is based on nationalistic thoughts in which the leader seeks to unite both countries due to the common language and other factors that bind the people from the two countries together.

According to exclusive nationalism, a person can only be a citizen of a country if they meet certain requirements. People who are not seen as belonging to the designated group are not accorded the same treatment as those who are. Islam, for instance, is regarded as Saudi Arabia's official religion. Therefore, non-Muslims cannot be regarded as citizens in this area[85]. Even if the categorisation is accurate, not all Muslims have always received the same treatment. Shia and other minority denominations suffer from prejudice and discrimination in the majority-Sunni society. People can face discrimination along political and economic lines as a result of the desire to categorise people precisely according to who is deemed a citizen and who is not. Additionally, this could deteriorate into violence as governments seek to assimilate minority groups forcibly. In China, for example, hundreds of thousands of Uighur Muslims were placed in detention centres and forced to learn Mandarin, renounce Islam, and pledge loyalty to the Chinese government[86]. In Iran, minority groups face persecution from the government. For instance, Baha'is are barred from attending universities because they possess and practice different religious views from the rest of the citizens[87]. In India, Hindu nationals advocate for preferential treatment of Hindus, failing to consider the rights and needs of Muslim Indians. In most extreme cases, nationalism has been cited as having caused genocide and targeted mass killings of specific groups of people.

Economic nationalism is a concept that allows governments to promote domestic control of the economy by preserving jobs and other economic privileges for nationals only. Nations practising this kind of nationalism seek to promote local industries while putting gaps in imports and oppose free international trade [88]. These strategies are aimed at protecting local industries from global competition. Thus, governments implement protectionist policies, including subsidies, tariffs, and import quotas. Such strategies could harm the country's citizens by increasing the overall prices of goods resulting in the need for citizens to bear the additional costs. Additionally, this makes it difficult for local industries to compete on international fronts based on retaliation from other nations through the imposition of tariffs and quotas, resulting in their inability to sell their products are competitive prices across international boundaries.

Nationalism in a Global Era

Following the world wars, countries came together to ensure that such horrific conflicts never occurred again. As a result, they founded international organisations including the United Nations, International Monetary Fund, and World Bank, which served as the foundation for the liberal world order. These organisations have the responsibility of preventing the violent tendencies of nationalism by establishing worldwide platforms for collaboration in order to advance overall security and economic development. The successful and peaceful coexistence of nations and governments around the world has been credited to these institutions. Recent developments and dynamics in the world have resulted in rising movements and cries for national independence. These include stagnating wages, rising income inequalities, and job losses associated with factors in the business operating environment, such as technological changes.

Similarities between Nationalism and Patriotism

Patriotism and nationalism cover aspects associated with the love for one's country. In the case of patriotism, the love is expressed and directed towards one's *Patria,* that is, one's country. For nationalism, on the other hand, love is expressed towards one's nation based on individuals' ethnic and cultural identity. Nationalism and patriotism are therefore brought together due to a common set of beliefs and attitudes exhibited to one's origin in the form of descent and with people having the same shared values, beliefs, and cultures.

Patriotism and nationalism are not concepts based on fixed natures. The relativity of the terms varies from region to region and between individuals, thus making it challenging to differentiate them in absolute terms. This, therefore, means that the concepts are related based on their connotations and resonances and touch on how people relate with their fatherlands, the country, and their nations[89]. Additionally, the political languages of the two terms do not fully overlap, thus resulting in the need to consider them together.

Patriotism and nationalism can be closely linked to the tendency of people to form and sustain civic engagements. For liberal democracies, there is a need for citizens to be committed and active. Patriotism is therefore crucial in gaining the engagement of citizens as expressed in their love and commitment towards their nation. Patriotism is a crucial factor in the nourishment of civic engagements within nations[90]. The concept helps in generating feelings of solidarity and mutual responsibility across the boundaries of selected identity groups. Patriotism is also associated with the sense of responsibility for one's country over the disengagement of government actions. While for nationalists, such attachments are associated with feelings of accomplishment and fulfilment, the patriots could exhibit feelings of shame, outrage, and anger over the actions of their government against others. As such, the patriots are likely to team up in opposing national policies that cause harm to others considered as a minority group.

Patriotism and nationalism also work together in providing support for redistributive social policies. For such policies to be considered legitimate and accepted in totality, there is a need to gain solidarity and mutual responsibility among citizens. Additionally, the language of nationhood has been considered crucial in fostering the integration of immigrants within communities.

Differences between Nationalism and Patriotism

Patriotism focuses on celebrating individuals as constituents of the country, as expressed by the patriots' love. In some instances, patriotism has been closely linked to xenophobia. Patriotism covers the affection for one's country or group, loyalty to the institutions, and a zeal for its defence. On the other hand, xenophobia focuses on disliking a stranger or an individual who does not belong to a specific group. Here, there is increased resistance to admitting one who does not belong to the group based on the differentiating characteristics[91]. Nationalism, on the other hand, tends to suppress individuals and citizens in a country by exalting the nation far beyond its constituents. This means that patriotism recognizes individuals and their role and loyalty to the country. It requires citizens to sacrifice all for the sake of their nation with their interests considered subordinate to national interests. Nationalistic thoughts strengthen the power and perpetuity of a nation over its subjects through the establishment of states as guided by laws and frameworks.

Examples include the expression of nationalism in the form of fascism in Italy and Nazism in Germany and Croatia during WW2 and the civil war in ex-Yugoslavia. Leaders during such times used economic and political turmoil associated with wars and strife in the early 20th century to subdue the interests of individual citizens to those of the nation. These leaders established an idea that glorified them and was justified by the identity and belongingness of individuals to a nation as well as the overriding interest of a nation resulting in absolute loyalty for the leaders. Consequently, the nation stood for the people's interests by putting them in the interests and passion of the nation. This ideology was further clarified by twentieth-century historians and scholars who explained it in terms of dictatorship through which dictators made individuals believe that they were loyal to their nations by exalting their leadership. This was exemplified in the twentieth-century world war, especially among the Nazi party officials in Germany[92]. The party was founded on the idea of the superiority of the German race Aryan over others. There was an increasing need to consider the Aryan race as the most superior of all other nations regarding intellectual, political, cultural, and military powers. Nazis, therefore, used violence as an instrument for nationalism, forcing others to submit to the ruling race and power.

Therefore, the essential differences between the two terms lie in the fact that patriotism is characterized by acceptance, human values, coexistence, and love for one's country for its own sake. Nationalism, on the other hand, covers aspects of power, prestige, strength, unity, and pride regarding the relationship with others. This concept promotes loyalty to one's ethnic descent while rejecting minorities considered inferior and objectionable to the ruling category.

Nationalism covers and combines the aspects of patriotism and xenophobia, resulting in a distinctive style of politics. According to French leader Charles de Gaulle, patriotism covers an individual's love for one country, with nationalism, covers the hate for people other than your own[93]. According to Albert Einstein, nationalism is considered an infantile thing, such as measles to humankind. This sickness is characterized by the tendency of persons to dissolve their individuality within this infantile while rejecting those who do not belong there. Accordingly, this is considered a bimodal alienation where members are engulfed within the group while isolating those outside it[94]. Here an individual is subordinated to a nation's collective objectives with those individuals outside the group being despised for not belonging within the nation.

Nationalism blames challenges faced in society squarely on outsiders. At first, the ideology uses an ethnic yardstick to classify people as belonging or not belonging to the leading group. Consequently, treatment for people within the group or nation is treated more superior to those outside it. In its extreme forms, nationalism calls for the creation of enemies of those not considered part of a nation based on specific identification criteria. Consequently, there is an increasing likelihood of defeat and domination over those excluded from the nation.

This was the case with the Nazi uprising and revolutions in ancient Germany. This begins with creating categories of individuals characterised by *us* versus *them* ideologies. Consequently, the ruling category de-individualises people as the tendency to consider people from different ethnographic backgrounds as outsiders who do not deserve the treatment accorded to individuals classified as part of the nation or group with favourable characteristics[95]. Further aggravation of the concept results in the dehumanisation of the people in which those classified as not belonging to the group are reduced to non-human status, being denied primary human considerations such as respect, decency, and in some cases, life as in the case of Nazism in Germany.

George Orwell presents thoughts around nationalism to create awareness about the consequences of such thoughts on the overall well-being of individuals within established state and national borders. Orwell recognizes that nationalistic thoughts revolve around competitive advantage for one's nation as characterized by individuals thinking about victories, humiliations, and triumphs whenever their nations are mentioned or involved with others. To a nationalist, every event is considered a demonstration for their side of the divide to upgrade and show their domination over the rival side. Orwell also notes while nationalism has been considered a factor that unites people, its danger lies in the fact that it unites a group of people against others[96]. This came at a time when nationalism had been attributed to its association with strives and wars between nations, resulting in the loss of lives and property. At this time, the writer noted that nationalism could be categorised as a power-hungered concept fuelled by self-deception.

Orwell also noted that nationalism failed to meet humanity's ethical and moral standards. While nationalists condemned outrages by others, they excused those done on their own or within their boundaries against others considered enemies. Thus, nationalists live by double standards, condemning adverse actions by others and praising and glorifying them when done by themselves[97.] Nationalism in its extreme forms has resulted in instances of warfare between nations, genocide between ethnic groups and racial extermination as characterised by the fights of us against them. These cases have been reported in areas such as Yugoslavia, Georgia, Rwanda, Iraq, and so on where the classification of people into specific groups based on particular classification criteria has resulted in the need to wipe out those considered outsiders to the ruling class of the majority group. Often NATO and the UN somehow instead of keeping peace managed to turn verbal conflicts into serious wars without paying any consequences.

An analysis by scholars on the nationalism ideology and the related concepts has resulted in identifying significant elements of the ideology. These include an increasing focus on national unity among individuals considered to belong to a nation. Consequently, individuals categorised as belonging to a nation must show exclusive loyalty to the nation while striving to attain national freedom over individual passions and needs. Other features of nationalists include the passion for distinctiveness and exclusiveness for a nation and the increasing focus on prestige and honour for a nation. This could easily translate into the urge and need for domination over others considered as weaker groups and nations.

While both nationalism and patriotism express relationships between individuals and their communities, differences exist because nationalism emphasizes the unity of individuals based on their cultural past together with the inclusion of language and heritage. In contrast, patriotism is based on love towards people, emphasising values and beliefs. According to Orwell, patriotism covers aspects of belongingness to a specified part of the world, believing that that is the best part of the world to live in[98]. Yet patriots do not have any interest in pushing other people. Consequently, the concept is exhibited in both military and cultural defence.

On the other hand, nationalism may not be easily separated from the wish to rule others. Here, the purpose of every nationalist has been captured as the provision of more power and reputation for the nation instead of themselves. While nationalism is considered the foundation for establishing nationals, it could be destructive in the long run, especially for nation-states and multiple ethnic structures. Patriotism provides conspicuous and excellent grounds for allowing people to unite for the nation's good.

Concerns have been raised regarding the ability of individuals to express their love for their country even in the face of terrorism. Here, scholars and researchers debated the aspects of national pride in the face of terrorism following the 9/11 attacks in the United States. They were sceptical about whether the expression ion national pride was related to ethnocentric and xenophobic expressions towards others[99]. It would not be easy for individuals to express their love for their nations as defined through the use of the word patriotism without also expressing aspects of nationalism as defined by the tendency of individuals to accept their national, state, and political authorities based on the belief that these were superior and dominant compared to others.

In theory, patriotism has often been considered as an affective attachment to one's group without affecting one's feelings towards those considered as not belonging to the group. Nationalism, on the other hand, is an explicit out–of–group antipathy. Here, there is an increased likelihood for individuals to show hostility and aggressiveness toward those considered as not belonging to the group.

An analysis of factors related to the two concepts shows that the terms are distinguishable. A different cluster of attitudes is related to the positive and critical appreciation of one's country and its symbols as expressed in the form of patriotism. On the other hand, different factors contribute to classifying people into two groups, 'us' versus 'them' as best characterized by the 'my country right or wrong' slogan. These factors are, however, related based on the fact that all include a positive in-group evaluation and consideration.

The social identity of the concepts shows that in-group and out-group derogations are not necessarily bundled together. This means that the presence of one does not necessarily mean the presence of the other and vice versa. Research has shown that an increase in the likelihood for individuals to identify themselves with those considered of the same group leads to negative attitudes and treatment of outsiders only when such minority groups or outsiders pose a threat to the in-group. Returning to the example of the flag display in the face of terrorism, this could have been considered a show of patriotism for individuals who felt less threatened by terrorism. To those who the outcomes of the terror activities had threatened, however, the flying of the American flag was considered an expression of nationalism or a complex blend of nationalism and patriotism while many countries around the world consider the American flag as a flag of modern terrorism.

In the face of terrorism, there have been propositions that nationalistic thoughts and actions could rise. The 9/11 terrorism resulted in the establishment of the Patriot Act and the increasing likelihood on the part of the government at various levels to sacrifice some of the prevailing civic liberties to fight terrorism[100]. This has been thought of as a crucial factor that could lead people toward particular forms of nationalism that could significantly influence the functionality of liberal democracies.

Scholars and researchers have applied various criteria to distinguish between the two terms. According to Lord Acton, the two concepts can be categorised as the affection and instinct an individual expresses for their country versus the moral relations towards their homeland. Therefore, nationality relates to the connection an individual has and expresses towards their race based on their natural and physical characteristics. At the same time, patriotism covers the level of awareness of citizens regarding their moral duties towards political establishments and the community. These classifications and definitions contrast with those put forth by Elie Kedourie in the twentieth century, where he expressed nationalism as a fully fledged political and philosophical doctrine regarding nations as the basic human unit, enabling individuals to obtain freedom and fulfillment[101]. According to this scholar, patriotism represented the sentimental affection for individuals toward their fatherlands.

George Orwell, on the other hand, differentiated the two terms based on their association with power. Nationalism covers the aggressive attitudes and actions in defence of one nation with patriotism covering the defence attitudes toward one's nation and homeland. Regarding patriotism, an individual defends their nation as being the best place without the need to push others into accepting their communities as the best. This distinction places the two concepts at par with their distinction based on the strength of love and special concerns individuals feel towards their countries and the degree of identification towards one's homeland. Patriotism enables individuals to express their feelings towards their homelands to reasonable degrees and without ill thoughts. In nationalism, such feelings are rampant, causing one to think badly of others and misbehave towards them.

World Citizenship

Opponents of nationalism and patriotism feel that individuals should identify themselves as citizens of the world instead of limiting themselves to national boundaries. Diogenes the Cynic is the first proponent of this line of thought, proudly categorising himself as the 'citizen of the world.' By this, he refused to be defined by his local origins and group memberships, instead defining himself in more universal aspirations and concerns[102]. The stoics took up this proposition, further building on the concept of world citizenship by proposing that people dwell in the local communities of birth and the global community, the community of human argument and aspirations. The larger community should influence our actions and decisions. When talking about justice, the proponent of world citizenship held that they should be regarded as fellow neighbours and citizens despite their communities of origin and descent. Deliberations and decisions should be based on the fact that they are first human problems, not problems arising from particular national identities.

Thinking as a global citizen tends to do away with the comfort of patriotism and the limitation of nationalism, calling individuals to see their ways of life from the view of justice and the need to do good to all. The stoics held on to the proposition that individuals needed not to allow differences in nationality or class, ethnic membership, and other such classifications to erect barriers between human beings. Instead, an emphasis was based on the need to recognize humanity, giving it the fundamental ingredients of morality, reasoning, allegiance, and respect. The stoics claim that individuals should give their first allegiance to no mere form of government or temporal power but a moral community composed of the humanity of all human beings[103]. In the face of globalisation and the immigration of individuals across national boundaries, there is a need to look at these propositions and determine whether they could support achieving the peaceful coexistence of people with diverse characteristics while sharing the same national boundaries.

Global governance requires that individuals exercise democracy in decision-making and all other processes and frameworks to ensure order and peaceful coexistence. Democracy, on the other hand, requires that leaders establish a system that provides people with a voice in making decisions that affect them while providing mechanisms through which leaders are held accountable. Opponents cite the increased fears of authoritarian imposition of a uniform system of governance, yet situations and circumstances within national boundaries vary from place to place. They propose the need for an international consensus to be flexible, dynamic, and minimalistic while respecting the virtue of existing pluralism. This calls for individuals to extend their loyalties beyond ethnicity, religion, community, and nations to the human race. This has and may not be achieved based on divisions already exhibited within communities and nations, making it difficult for leaders to agree on a global perspective of handling various issues.

Conclusion

Nationalism and patriotism have often been used interchangeably, yet differences exist. While the two concepts overlap based on efforts to differentiate them from the points of view of various scholars and philosophers, there have been efforts to obtain acceptable and universal definitions and applications of the two concepts while talking about humanity and tackling issues and strife that have been associated with them. The first point in establishing the relationship between the two terms is that they require loyalty, allegiance, and love from citizens for leaders and political institutions created within countries and national boundaries. For patriotism, the love towards one country is defensive while nationalists are aggressive in expressing their love and loyalty towards their nations. Extremities of the concepts have, however, been associated with wars, genocides, and ethnic cleansing as communities and nations seek to push out of their borders those who are categorized and considered outsiders. The concept of global citizenship has been proposed requiring individuals to consider themselves as citizens of the world first before considering their local nations and factors of descent. Such has not gained popularity as political leaders seek to promote and achieve the needs of their citizens first before thinking in terms of the global needs of humanity.

References

1. Poole, R (2016) 'Patriotism and nationalism', *Patriotism.* Routledge, pp 137–154.

2. Kwak, J H (2014) "Patriotism and Nationalism", 'Republican Patriotism in the Northeast Asian Context', *Patriotism in East Asia,* edited by Jun-Hyeok Kwak and Koichiro Matsuda. London: Routledge, pp 28–45.

3. Bell, D A and Bell, D A (2009) *The Cult of the Nation in France: Inventing Nationalism, 1680–1800.* Harvard University Press.

4. Primoratz, I (2009) 'Patriotism'.

5. Robertson, R (2017) 'Cosmopolitanism, Patriotism, and Nationalism in the German and Austrian Enlightenment', *Enlightenment Cosmopolitanism.* Routledge, pp 12–30.

6. Bar-Tal, D (1993) 'Patriotism as fundamental beliefs of group members', *Politics and the Individual,* 3(2), pp 45–62.

7. Scalia, L J (1998) 'Who deserves political influence? How liberal ideals helped justify mid nineteenth-century exclusionary policies', *American Journal of Political Science,* pp 349–376.

8.   Nathanson, S (1993) *Patriotism, Morality, and Peace.* Rowman & Littlefield.

9.   Kodelja, Z (2011) 'Is education for patriotism morally required, permitted or unacceptable?', *Studies in Philosophy and Education*, 30(2), pp 127–140.

10. Hertz, F (1940) 'The nature of nationalism'. *Soc F, 19*, p 409.

11. Ikuenobe, P (2010) 'Citizenship and patriotism', *Public Affairs Quarterly*, 24(4), pp 297–318.

12. Kleinig, J (2015) 'The virtue in patriotism', *The Ethics of Patriotism: A Debate*, pp 19–47.

13. Orr, D W (2012) *The Last Refuge: Patriotism, Politics, and the Environment in an Age of Terror.* Island Press.

14. Nathanson, S (2020) 'Moderate patriotism', *Handbook of Patriotism*, pp 141–161.

15. Baron, M and Rogers, T (2020) 'Patriotism and impartiality', *Handbook of Patriotism*, pp 409–427.

16. Primoratz, I (2008) 'Patriotism and morality: Mapping the terrain', *Journal of Moral Philosophy*, 5(2), pp 204–226.

17. Goode, J P (2016) 'Love for the motherland:(or why cheese is more patriotic than Crimea)', *Russian Politics*, 1(4), pp 418–449.

18. Parker, C S (2010) 'Symbolic versus blind patriotism: Distinction without difference?', *Political Research Quarterly*, 63(1), pp 97–114.

19. Staub, E (1997) 'Blind versus constructive patriotism: Moving from embeddedness in the group to critical loyalty and action'.

20. Nathanson, S (1993) *Patriotism, Morality, and Peace.* Rowman & Littlefield.

21. Swann Jr, W B, Gómez, Á, Dovidio, J F, Hart, S, and Jetten, J (2010) 'Dying and killing for one's group: Identity fusion moderates responses to intergroup versions of the trolley problem', *Psychological science*, 21(8), pp 1176–1183.

22. Shyrokov, S (2019) 'Modern investigation concepts of Patriotism in the foreign scientific research', *Public Administration and Local Government*, 4 (43), pp 14–19.

23. Sardoč, M (2017) 'The anatomy of patriotism', *Anthropological Notebooks*, 23(1).

24. Whetham, D (2016) 'My Country, Right or Wrong: If the Cause is Just, is Anything Allowed?', *The Ashgate Research Companion to Military Ethics.* Routledge, pp 303–314.

25. Nathanson, S (2020) 'Moderate patriotism', *Handbook of Patriotism*, pp 141–161.

26. Bragg, B (2007) *The Progressive Patriot: A Search for Belonging.* Random House.

27. Merry, M S (2009) 'Patriotism, history and the legitimate aims of American education', *Educational Philosophy and Theory*, 41(4), pp 378–398.

28. Vogt, S (2012) 'The First World War, German Nationalism, and the Transformation of German Zionism', *The Leo Baeck Institute Year Book*, 57(1), pp 267–291.

29. Forchtner, B and Kølvraa, C (2015) 'The nature of nationalism: Populist radical right parties on countryside and climate', *Nature and Culture*, 10(2), pp 199–224.

30. Brubaker*, R (2004) 'In the name of the nation: Reflections on nationalism and patriotism', *Citizenship Studies*, 8(2), pp 115–127.

31. Smith, A D (1991) 'National Identity'. New York, London: Penguin Books.

32. Yack, B (2018) 'Popular sovereignty and nationalism', *Relocating Sovereignty*. Routledge, pp. 205–224.

33. Stilz, A (2011) 'Nations, states, and territory', *Ethics*, 121(3), pp 572–601.

34. Goodblatt, D (2006) *Elements of Ancient Jewish Nationalism.* Cambridge University Press.

35. Richmond, O P (2002) 'States of sovereignty, sovereign states, and ethnic claims for international status', *Review of International Studies*, 28(2), pp 381–402.

36. Sassen, S (1996) *Losing Control?: Sovereignty in the Age of Globalization.* Columbia University Press.

37. Eriksen, T H (2002) *Ethnicity and Nationalism: Anthropological Perspectives.* Pluto Press.

38. Brubaker, R (2009) 'Ethnicity, race, and nationalism', *Annual Review of Sociology*, pp 21–42.

39. Berdún, M M G, Guibernau, M, and Rex, J (eds) (2010) *The Ethnicity Reader: Nationalism, Multiculturalism and Migration.* Polity.

40. Schnee, W (2001) 'Nationalism: A review of the literature,' *Journal of Political & Military Sociology*, pp 1–18.

41. Breuilly, J (1993) *Nationalism and the State*. Manchester University Press.

42. Conversi, D (2010) 'Ideology and nationalism', *Routledge Handbook of Ethnic Conflict*. Routledge, pp 44–61.

43. Penrose, J (2002) 'Nations, states and homelands: territory and territoriality in nationalist thought', *Nations and Nationalism*, 8(3), pp 277–297.

44. Patten, A. (1999) 'The autonomy argument for liberal nationalism', *Nations and Nationalism*, 5(1), pp 1–17.

45. Leerssen, J (2006) 'Nationalism and the Cultivation of Culture', *Nations and Nationalism*, 12(4), pp 559–578.

46. Muller, J Z (2008) 'Us and them: The enduring power of ethnic nationalism', *Foreign Affairs*, pp 18–35.

47. Rashiduzzaman, M (2018) 'Bangladesh: MUSLIM Identity, Secularism, and the Politics of Nationalism', *Religion and Politics in the Developing World: Explosive Interactions*. Routledge, pp 128–142.

48. Tamir, Y (2019) 'Not so civic: is there a difference between ethnic and civic nationalism?', *Annual Review of Political Science*, 22, pp 419–434.

49. Lecours, A (2000) 'Ethnic and civic nationalism: towards a new dimension', *Space and Polity*, 4(2), pp 153–166.

50. Springs, J A (2015) 'A Tale of Two Islamophobias the Paradoxes of Civic Nationalism in Contemporary Europe and the United States', *Soundings: An Interdisciplinary Journal*, 98(3), pp 289–321.

51. Adorno, T W and Pickford, H W (1997) 'Opinion delusion society', *The Yale Journal of Criticism*, 10(2), pp 227–245.

52. Smith, A D and Smith, A (2013) *Nationalism and Modernism*. Routledge.

53. Van der Veer, P (1994) *Religious Nationalism: Hindus and Muslims in India*. University of California Press.

54. Knight, D B (1982) 'Identity and territory: geographical perspectives on nationalism and regionalism', *Annals of the Association of American Geographers*, 72(4), pp 514–531.

55. Tamir, Y (1995) *Liberal Nationalism*. Princeton University Press.

56. Auer, S (2004) *Liberal Nationalism in Central Europe*. Routledge.

57. Roshwald, A (2002) *Ethnic Nationalism and the Fall of Empires: Central Europe, the Middle East and Russia, 1914–23*. Routledge.

58. Trone, E (2017) 'The Double-Edged Sword: The Development of Reactionary yet Revolutionary Chinese Nationalism', *Flame Board*.

59. Waldron, A (2003) *From War to Nationalism: China's Turning Point, 1924–1925*. Cambridge University Press.

60. Eley, G (1991) *Reshaping the German Right: Radical Nationalism and Political Change after Bismarck*. University of Michigan Press.

61. Gal, A, Leoussi, A S, and Smith, A D (eds.) (2010) *The Call of the Homeland: Diaspora Nationalisms, past and present* (Vol. 9). Brill.

62. Rabinovitch, S (ed) (2012) *Jews and Diaspora Nationalism: Writings on Jewish Peoplehood in Europe and the United States*. UPNE.

63. McNeill, W H (2019) 'Polyethnicity and national unity in world history', *Polyethnicity and National Unity in World History*. University of Toronto Press.

64. Rowe, M (2013) 'The French revolution, Napoleon, and nationalism in Europe', *The Oxford Handbook of the History of Nationalism*.

65. Dann, O and Dinwiddy, J (eds) (1988) *Nationalism in the Age of the French Revolution*. A&C Black.

66. Lawrence, P (2016) *Nationalism: History and Theory*. Routledge.

67. Smith, A D (2013) *Nationalism: Theory, Ideology, History*. John Wiley & Sons.

68. Berberoglu, B (1995) *The National Question: Nationalism, Ethnic Conflict, and Self-Determination in the 20th Century*. Temple University Press.

69. Denitch, B D (1996) *Ethnic Nationalism: The Tragic Death of Yugoslavia*. University of Minnesota Press.

70. Sutherland, C (2011) *Nationalism in the Twenty-First Century: Challenges and Responses*. Macmillan International Higher Education.

71. Vhutuza, E and Ngoshi, H (2008) Nationalism or Supra-Nationalism in the 21st Century?', *Orientation et Objectifs*, 70(1), 176.

72. Triandafyllidou, A (2020) Nationalism in the 21st century: Neo-tribal or plural?', *Nations and Nationalism*, 26(4), pp 792–806.

73. Statkus, N (2019) 'The role of nationalism in the 21ˢᵗ-century system of international relations', *Lithuanian Annual Strategic Review*, 17, pp 125–156.

74. Malešević, S and Trošt, T P (2007) 'Nation-State and Nationalism', *The Blackwell Encyclopedia of Sociology*, pp 1–9.

75. Irawan, A D (2020) 'Nationalism in a State Based on Pancasila', *Petita: Jurnal Kajian Ilmu Hukum Dan Syariah*, 5(2), pp 133–144.

76. Sugito, N, Aulia, R, and Rukmana, L (2021, February) 'Pancasila as the Establishing Ideology of Nationalism Indonesian Young Generation', *1ˢᵗ International Conference on Character Education (ICCE 2020)*. Atlantis Press, pp 177–182.

77. Periwal, S (ed) (1995) *Notions of Nationalism*. Central European University Press.

78. Mann, M (2013) 'The role of nationalism in the two world wars', *Nationalism and War*, pp 172–196.

79. Biersack, J, and O'Leary, S (2014) 'The geopolitics of Russia's annexation of Crimea: narratives, identity, silences, and energy', *Eurasian Geography and Economics*, 55(3), pp 247–269.

80. Harris, E (2020) 'What is the role of nationalism and ethnicity in the Russia–Ukraine crisis?', *Europe-Asia Studies*, 72(4), pp 593–613.

81. Kuzio, T (2015) 'Competing Nationalisms, Euromaidan, and the Russian-Ukrainian Conflict', *Studies in Ethnicity and Nationalism*, 15(1), pp 157–169.

82. Laruelle, M (2015) 'Russia as a "Divided nation" from compatriots to Crimea: A contribution to the discussion on nationalism and foreign policy', *Problems of Post-Communism*, 62(2), pp 88–97.

83. Magocsi, P R (2016) 'The roots of Ukrainian nationalism', *The Roots of Ukrainian Nationalism*. University of Toronto Press.

84. Kolstø, P, and Blakkisrud, H (2016) *The New Russian Nationalism*. Edinburgh University Press.

85. Partrick, N (2013) 'Nationalism in the Gulf states', *The Transformation of the Gulf*. Routledge, pp 66–84.

86. Hyer, E (2006) 'China's policy towards Uighur nationalism', *Journal of Muslim Minority Affairs*, 26(1), pp 75–86.

87. Zabihi-Moghaddam, S (2016) 'State-Sponsored Persecution of Baha'is in the Islamic Republic of Iran', *Contemporary Review of the Middle East*, 3(2), pp 124–146.

88. Helleiner, E, and Pickel, A (eds) (2005) *Economic Nationalism in a Globalizing World*. Cornell University Press.

89. Wright, E 'Patriotism and Nationalism: A Question of Epistemology?'

90. Uslaner, E M and Conley, R S (2003) 'Civic engagement and particularized trust: The ties that bind people to their ethnic communities', *American Politics Research*, 31(4), pp 331–360.

91. Hjerm, M (2001) 'Education, xenophobia and nationalism: A comparative analysis', *Journal of Ethnic and Migration Studies*, 27(1), pp 37–60.

92. Fritzsche, P (1998) *Germans into Nazis*. Harvard University Press.

93. Turygina, N (2016) 'Patriotism among Russian emigrants in Europe during the Second World war', *3rd International Multidisciplinary Scientific Conference on Social Sciences and Arts SGEM 2016*, pp 481–488.

94. Demuijnck, G (2005) 'Poverty as a human rights violation and the limits of nationalism', *Real World Justice*. Springer, Dordrecht, pp 65–83.

95. Mackey, E (2013) 'Anthropological Perspectives on World Issues', *Introductory Readings in Anthropology*, p 380.

96. Orwell, G (2018) *Notes on Nationalism*. Penguin UK.

97. Donskis, L (2006) 'Nationalism: The Center Ground', *Transitions Online*, (02/07).

98. Rossi, J P (2001) 'George Orwell's concept of patriotism', *Modern Age*, 43(2), p 128.

99. Hutcheson, J, Domke, D, Billeaudeaux, A, and Garland, P (2004) 'US national identity, political elites, and a patriotic press following September 11. *Political Communication*, 21(1), pp 27–50.

100. Etzioni, A (2005) *How Patriotic Is the Patriot Act?: Freedom versus Security in the Age of Terrorism*. Routledge.

101. Kitromilides, P M (2005) 'Elie Kedourie's contribution to the study of nationalism', *Middle Eastern Studies*, 41(5), pp 661–663.

102. Nussbaum, M (1994) 'Patriotism and cosmopolitanism', *The Cosmopolitan Reader*, pp 155–162.

103. Conversi, D (2000) 'Cosmopolitanism and nationalism', *Encyclopaedia of Nationalism*, pp 34–39.

CHAPTER 2

Psychology of Nationalism

Nationalists hold solid attitudes and beliefs about their people and others. Such individuals have often felt a strong and passionate attachment to their nations, sometimes even acting cruelly towards their perceived enemies. According to Searle White in his book, 'On the Psychology of Nationalism, the 'us' versus 'them' mentality has adverse effects on others considered outside a nation's boundaries (Kećmanović, 2003). According to the social-psychological perspectives on human behaviour, nationalist thoughts are attributed to the aspects of attachment and identity.

The world is composed of countless species, with the human race having more than seven billion members. Looking at this from one perspective, there could be natural borders characterised by the existence of mountains and seas. On the other hand, borders between nations are characterised by abstraction and imaginary boundaries established as a result of agreements or conflicts between people that have been used to categorise humans into various groups (Donnan and Wilson, 2021).

Rusty Schweickart, an Apollo 9 space mission member, explained how the earth looked from space. His tour into the space changed his perspective regarding national boundaries and the conduct of individuals based on their belongingness to a nation. Having been brought up to think about nations and borders between different nationalities, he could now see the world from above. Here, there were no boundaries, and thus he felt part of everything and everyone. Looking at the world from above, he says, 'One could not imagine how many borders and boundaries you cross, again and again, and you don't even see them.' According to Schweikhart's perspective, it is apparent that we belong to the earth rather than a nation and a species rather than a nationality. Even though we feel distinct and different from each other, we have a common source of origin (White, 1998). According to the evolutionary theory, the human species existed in Eastern Africa around 200,000 years ago, migrating out into the rest of the world in waves.

Terror Management Theory

With the same ancestral origin, it is a wonder that the human race is now divided into nationalities with different norms, customs, behaviours, and values. One psychological theory that has been applied in justifying the existence of different nationalities is the terror management theory, which cites insecurity and anxiety as contributing factors to dividing and regrouping people based on common characteristics such as ancestry. According to this theory, when people experience tension and anxiety, they become more concerned with nationalism, success, and status (Greenberg et al, 2008). There is an increasing tendency for individuals to cling to labels of identity while seeking to defend themselves against insecurities.

Research on the terror management theory has been conducted to determine the attitudes of individuals towards those with different political attitudes compared to their own. Researchers have analysed mortality salience towards those who support or threaten one's cultural worldview. Such studies showed that elements of physical aggression towards persons who derogated one's political orientation existed (Burke, Martens, and Faucher, 2010).

According to this theory, nationalism has been known to grow and thrive during crises and uncertainty. Additionally, poverty and economic instability have been cited as crucial in increasing antagonistic feelings among people and leading to ethnic conflicts. As the sense of insecurity increases among people, a more vital need for conceptual labels to strengthen a group's sense of identity and belongingness develops. This result in the growing impulse towards security as a result of belongingness to a group that shares conventions and beliefs. As such, it is believed that people who feel the most robust sense of separation and the highest levels of insecurity and anxiety are likely to exhibit nationalism, racism, and fundamentalist religion.

Fallacy of Nationalism

People often think that Schweikhart's perspective lacks a sense of accuracy from the earth since the reality is that individuals live as different national groups with diverse traditions and borders within them. The concept of belongingness to distinct national and racial groups has obtained criticism based on its lack of foundation and basis in seeking to divide individuals into groups and nations. Looking at this objectively, an estimated seven billion humans live in different parts of the planet's habitable land. Borders between people, as explained by Schweikhart, are just abstractions and imaginary boundaries created to benefit specific groups of individuals.

A linguistic assessment of the diverse language groups exposes similarities in language structures and vocabularies even for individuals who are geographically apart. Scientists have identified fundamental vocabularies and grammatical structures shared among human races, suggesting that language in the human race could have originated from one human language. This points to the proposition that the human race originated from the horn of Africa between 200,000 and 300,000 years ago, migrating to the rest of the world over time.

An objective analysis of the theory of common origin points out the commonality in linguistics in geographic origin for the human species (Smith, 2013). Therefore, the concept of different races is a fallacy since the human race is considered one species that moved to different places and developed different traits due to environmental conditions encountered upon migration.

The concept of nationalism is also considered a fallacy. The migration theory shows that as individuals moved and settled in various distinct regions, they developed some traits due to the environmental conditions characterizing these physical locations (De Genova, 2013). Such groups integrated and organized themselves into cohesive groups, operating under the same administrative and social systems. With the belief that humans have the same identity and origin, it is a wonder that the categorisation of individuals based on national boundaries has been the order of the day. Humans tend to separate themselves into groups that have been characterized by conflicts and competition with each other.

Since the migration of humans based on their history, they have often lived in tribes. Nevertheless, it would not be correct to assume that people are identified exclusively according to their tribes and that people within an identified tribe could treat others with hostility based on the fact that they do not belong to their group. It follows that the hunters and gatherers, groups that followed the lifestyle of prehistoric human beings, were fluid individuals changing membership and embracing others without much profiling and categorisation (McConvell, 2010). They used to visit each other, make marriage alliances and even switch group members. This is an indication, therefore, that nationalism is not an innate impulse inherited from our ancestors.

Psychology of Nationalism-Research Outcomes

The psychology of nationalism covers the tendency for individuals to identify with a given group due to common religious beliefs, family, and personal connections. The increasing tendency among human beings to belong to or associate with a particular group of people is considered a universal motive of human activity. Excessive usage of such connections and a sense of belongingness have resulted in nationalistic feelings among individuals, resulting in adverse effects and consequences on the well-being of individuals and groups (Brock and Atkinson, 2008). According to Erich Fromm (2013), individuals are considered political creatures who seek to join others like themselves from groups and associations. Consequently, the lifestyles of individuals within the same group are likely to be similar based on the presence and adherence to group norms and customers.

Psychologists have researched to evaluate the existence of conflicts and wars between groups of people, yet we all face similar and common challenges in our lives. From an outsider's point of view, some conflicts seem pointless. One could be tempted to ask the question, 'Why can't you just get along?' to the conflicting groups yet these nationalistic conflicts are not pointless to them. It has been established that various psychological reasons exist supporting the feelings of attachment to people and various causes to justify the injury and death of opponents and community members (Druckman, 2001).

In his book *The Psychology of Nationalism*, Joshua Searle-White begins with an experiment of placing students into groups. He gives them various assignments to be handled in the specified groups. One striking factor was the conduct of a group that was given powers to control the classroom door. The group prided itself in its identity, causing conflicts with the other three groups and constantly using its powers to get favourable outcomes over the others. The others groups were left desperate based on their inability to negotiate with the powerful groups branded as the Gatekeepers. The members of this group were branded as obstinate, uncompromising, and arrogant, yet they were smirking, laughing, and urging their representatives at the negotiation table to be more stubborn (Kećmanović, 2003).

Putting the students into groups and the resulting strife and conflicts produced outcomes similar to those experienced in nationalism. The Gatekeepers had developed a sense of group identity, feeling proud of their symbol and colour. They enjoyed a sense of group cohesiveness, humiliating and defeating the other groups. Throughout the semester, Joshua Searle-White noted that the Gatekeepers portrayed elements common in nationalistic conflicts. They sought to promote themselves, maximize their gains, and disparage the efforts of others.

While this was just an example, nationalistic conflicts are more severe and complex in the real world. Such conflicts affect the nation's political, economic, and historical existence as well as lives and property (Williams, 2001). Nations often fight over resources. Individuals who engage in nationalism carry solid attitudes and beliefs about their people, and others are often perceived as enemies. Such is passionate about defending the interests of their group to the extent of acting with great cruelty against their enemies.

The psychological evaluation of nationalism shows how individuals process information resulting in how they feel about themselves and others. Thoughts about oneself and others result in the categorisation of people into groups. While this is a helpful concept allowing individuals to go through life with ease in decisions making, it impacts how we treat others upon being placed into groups. Several aspects exist regarding the classification of people into groups. Potential characteristics include a common history, shared language, and culture (Bairner, 2001). The characteristic of belongingness and living in a specified part of the globe also lead to group formation. Nationalism in Western Europe and North America is attributed to individuals' sense of belonging and residence. People who moved to America automatically became US nationals. Here, belonging to a specified national group result from living in a particular area and being part of the specified political group and civic structures. Another categorizing aspect lies in an individual's lineage, religion, and language, more commonly referred to as the ethnic idea of national identity. Any intergroup boundaries existing here are associated with predictable attitudes and thinking patterns of individuals and groups.

Following the categorisation of people into a group, the aspects of attitude towards people belonging to and those outside a group arise.

People are likely to see the members of their group as moral, good, and strong, an aspect referred to as in-group favouritism. The tendency to describe one's group favourably than those considered outside the group is common and is considered a natural flow from categorisation (Verdery, 1993). Consequently, categorisation results in feelings of stereotyping for individuals categorised as out-group. Once an individual is categorised as part of a national group, they are considered to have the same qualities as all other individuals in the group. This concept is referred to as out-group homogenisation.

Stereotyping, as a result of the concepts discussed above, shapes how individuals treat and understand any new information about a group. Here, there is an increasing likelihood to consider the behaviour of one group member to be exhibiting the behaviours and conduct of all the other individuals categorised in the same group. Perception of out-groups is crucial in the cycle of conflict among people categorized under different nations. Perceiving individuals outside the group as untrustworthy, for example, has been cited as a crucial element in justifying violence and actions of aggression against others.

Outside devaluation refers to the tendency of an individual to devalue and exaggerate the actions and behaviours of those considered enemies of one's national group. Once there has been a devaluation of others groups as bad or evil, there is an increasing tendency to justify violence and aggression against them. The use of propaganda is common in group and national conflicts as individuals tend to form an image of their members against their enemies (Perdue et al., 1990). During World War I, groups were increasingly likely to devalue their opponents. People and groups described their opponents or enemies as aggressive, godless, greedy, uncivilised, and sadistic. More often than not, there were increasing tendencies to the dehumanisation of enemies.

Psychological Research on Conflicts

Various researchers have invested their time and resources in critically examining nationalism and aspects of group conflicts. One group of researchers attribute conflicts to the actions of a small number of extremists within a population while others believe that group aggression results from a natural competition of groups and individuals over resources.

A common feature among nationalists is riots and mob violence. Explanations of aspects of riots and hooliganism among an identified group of people can be attributed to the actions of a few individuals who stir or push the rioters into action. Elements of provocation from external forces have been cited as the driving forces for conflicts between communities and nations (Gerlach, 2010). In other cases, self-interest groups such as smugglers, criminals, and politicians have been at the forefront of instigating and supporting riots and violence for their selfish interests.

An assessment of such circumstances in the real-life situation points to the need for more focused efforts at answering questions on whether nationalist violence can be classified as the work of only a few extremists and whether some personality qualities inform the rates and level of violence and riots within national boundaries. In various circumstances, individuals have been led to war because of the underlying benefits, including looting of property, the use of war and conflicts by leaders to remain in power, and the associated propaganda that they are fighting a just war (Huszka, 2013). In secessionist wars, the benefits have often been associated with access to arms sales and the smuggling of various items across national borders. An assessment of many cases of violence and riots throughout history, however, does not point out the fact that all rioters and hooligans benefit from their actions. This points to the fact that some people could be psychologically more predisposed to hooliganism, extremism, and violence.

Extensive research on these aspects by a group of psychologists, including T W Adorno and his colleagues, was based on surveys. It showed that some individuals have personalities that are prone to see the world as a dangerous place with the need for people to fight themselves (Adorno, 2000). As such, the individuals categorised under this group were more likely to feel comfortable within societies with strict hierarchies to exhibit the position of one in society. The significant characteristics of these individuals revolved around feelings of ambivalence, especially towards their parents and close associates, high levels of morality, and the need for definiteness and the analysis of events outside one's control. These also believed in strong social order with clear lines of hierarchy and authority. As such, they possessed higher and more pronounced aspects of prejudice and ethnocentrism. This research provides insights regarding the feelings of individuals towards ambiguity and the extent to which they exhibit negative feelings towards other groups. This results in the availability of various groups based on the extent to which they support nationalism. Some individuals are more active than others in nationalistic struggles, thus acting as leaders in such activities. Other individuals, on the other hand, are likely to participate fully or partly in nationalistic movements.

Other factors that predispose individuals to actions of violence and conflicts include cultural and social conditions. Rapid social changes, unemployment, homelessness, and political conflicts have often been cited as crucial elements for conflicts among various population groups (Stewart, Holdstock, and Jarquin, 2002). These instances cause individuals to feel uncertain about the future. Consequently, they are likely to blame their current occurrences on minority groups within the population, thus justifying aggression and violence against such.

According to Staub (2012), various cultural qualities predispose societies to mass violence. These include the increasing sense among the majority that they deserve success over their opponents, as well as underlying insecurity and the history of out-group devaluations. Others include obedience to authority and the existence of monolithic political cultures.

Another psychological justification for group conflicts is closely linked to competition over resources. According to the realistic group conflict theory, group hostilities arise as groups compete for the same resources. The theory states that a conflict will arise whenever there are two or more groups of people seeking the same limited resources. This is also associated with negative stereotypes and beliefs and discrimination between groups. Such conflicts lead to animosity towards groups resulting in ongoing feuds (Brief et al, 2005). Identity is a crucial consideration in the psychological explanations for various national conflicts. Individuals are likely to indulge in wars and conflicts as they seek to define, strengthen, and protect the boundaries of identity.

Beyond Nationalism

According to psychology studies, people who experience high levels of well-being and a connection to others do not have a high sense of group identity. Individuals who have experienced various crises and turmoil have turned out with different perspectives on nationalism and a sense of belongingness. They have shifted to higher levels of human development due to a dramatic form of post-traumatic growth in which their lives are more meaningful, richer, and fulfilling. Research shows that such individuals exhibit a sense of appreciation and a heightened awareness of their surroundings. They develop a broader perspective associated with more intimate and authentic relationships (De Schutter, 2007). Such individuals start defining themselves in the form of belonging to the broader sense of humanity rather than nations, religions, and ideologies. They feel the same kinship with other humans rather than those of the same descent, ethnic, religious, and national groups. Such individuals identify themselves as global citizens, being members of the human race and inhabitants of the planet rather than nations characterised by boundaries.

According to basic cognitive development theories such as the Jean Piaget theory of child development, children undergo a socialisation process enabling them to move from the egocentric state to the socio-centric state (McLeod, 2007). Consequently, they build attachments to groups to meet their basic human needs. Accordingly, a nation becomes a social unit that fulfils individuals' economic, social-cultural, and political needs, giving them a sense of prestige, belongingness, and security. The sense of belonging, according to several psychologists, is crucial in human motivation. Hence national attachment has been considered crucial in helping individuals to construct their identity.

According to the social identity theory by Henri Tajfel, a person's identity is attributed to group status and belongingness. An individual's view of national superiority increases self-esteem, resulting in in-group favouritism and out-group devaluation (Islam, 2014). Accordingly, humans face the need to improve their sense of self by comparing themselves to others in *us* versus *them* mentality.

Other psychologists feel that the size of a nation and its military capabilities and experiences influences the nationalistic tendencies of its citizens. Accordingly, people in smaller countries face threats and insecurities from their neighbours and are prone to be nationalistic. These nationalistic feelings and insecurities seep into the individual level since people have been considered to draw self-esteem and status from their countries. They will likely react to such threats by displaying a sense of superiority.

It suffices to say that nationalistic thoughts are not entirely negative. According to other psychologists, nationalism, as expressed in the devotion to a nation, brings out the transcendent qualities in people and facilitates selflessness and courage as well as ideals. Some of the benefits accrued by individuals in the process of belonging to a group include enhanced self-esteem and loyalty resulting in more pride for the individual and the nation. According to Searle-White, nationalism unifies individuals across gender, political lines, and classes (Kećmanović, 2003).

Evolutionary Psychology

The concept of natural selection influences individual behaviour and action. Psychologists suggest that human behaviour is selected just like our physical traits. As humans evolve, various thoughts, behaviours, and qualities have been passed down through generations. Evolutionary psychological behaviour can be traced back to the hunter-and-gatherer ancestors and informs our natural tendencies to respond in a particular manner to various aspects and actions in our societies. While individuals often respond to a situation based on inherited characteristics, there is often a mismatch pitting individuals to juggle ancestral tendencies with the demands of modern-day living. Behaviours exhibited by people have been linked to self-preservation (Confer et al, 2010). Belongingness to a group is crucial for encouraging cooperation and the chances of survival for an identified group of individuals. As people within groups experience and perceive threats from the surrounding environment, they are likely to adopt the flight-or-fight concept preparing them to face danger or run from it.

Kin selection is another crucial component in evolutionary psychology that is likely to affect individuals' passion and need for belongingness to society. Hamilton established this theory to predict human altruism expressed towards kin of different proximity. The development of this theory showed that ethnic kinship was equivalent to the genetic variation between individuals. There was an increasing likelihood for ethnic kinships to be treated similarly to family kinships (Jones, 2018).

The theory interprets the actions of individuals in society. The behavioural universality of nepotism was considered a product of evolutionary history. Here, the rigours of natural selection, including the unreciprocated sharing of resources between individuals, were only viable when practised between close kin. According to various psychologists, ethnic groups are formed and practice unity since members consider themselves an extension of kin groups (Goetze and James, 2004). Other researchers show that solidarity among groups is based on family feelings. Additionally, ethnicity has been considered a crucial component in family resemblance, pointing out the fact that kinship is crucial in understanding the role of family structure in determining ethnic identity and explaining the intensity of conflicts between various ethnic groups.

People are likely to make sacrifices and favour those that belong to the same family and descent settings as themselves. This, according to psychologists, has been considered a crucial concept in the survival of people closely related to each other. These thoughts are, therefore, foundational to the nationalistic perspective and view towards the different treatment of in-group and out-of-the-group individuals.

The Savanna IQ-Interaction Hypothesis

Scholars and researchers have embarked on efforts to determine why some individuals are supportive of nationalistic thoughts while others are not. According to psychology today, the human brain is considered to have evolved over the years, being shaped by the pressures associated with survival and reproduction. This concept is crucial in assessing and understanding the origin of individual values and preferences. Accordingly, the Savannah principle was coined, relating the thoughts and human brain to circumstances and situations related to an individual's ancestral environment. According to the theory of the evolution of general intelligence, this intelligence evolved from domain-specific psychological adaptations to solve problems associated with evolution and demands for survival during these periods. The Savanna principle, therefore, links individuals' preferences and values to evolutionary tendencies aimed at solving evolutionarily novel problems (Dutton, 2013).

According to Kanazawa, the human mind was adapted to live in the African savannah more than 130,000 years ago during the Pleistocene period. As a result of the need to survive in such an environment, the human brain, including the brain's cognitive function, evolved to optimise the human ability to perform necessary tasks as vital at the time, including foraging. As such, Kanazawa stated that human brains likely face difficulty processing and dealing with entities not present in the ancestral environment (Kanazawa, 2009).

Accordingly, intelligence is considered a domain-specific adaptation developed in humans as they moved away from the savannah as a means of helping them to solve increasing problems and challenges associated with the novel problems encountered during the transition and evolution out of the first circumstances and environment. As individuals moved further from the savannah environment, there would be an increased likelihood that the savannah instinct would be helpful. Consequently, humans would more likely solve their problems by utilizing their intelligence rather than instincts.

The intelligence paradox also explains the exciting likelihood that people prefer the values they understand over their instincts. The more intelligent humans are, therefore, they are likely to adopt and espouse evolutionary novel values and forms of behaviour. Some aspects associated with novel evolutionary entities include individuals' ideas and lifestyles forming the basis for individuals' preferences and values. It would be difficult for individuals to value and prefer concepts they cannot truly comprehend. Consequently, nationalism considered a familiar evolutionary concept, can be considered and treated along these lines. As a result, less intelligent individuals are more likely to be nationalists than their more intelligent counterparts.

Brain Circuitry and Function

Basic principles of evolutionary psychology underlie the decisions and actions by humans predicting the resultant outcomes regarding association with and treatment of others. One fundamental principle lies with the brain as a physical system that functions by instructing a person to behave appropriately by adopting the presenting environmental factors. The brain's neural circuitry is crucial in supporting individuals in solving problems in a suitable manner. The specific manner in which the brain circuits are likely to react is based on the elements of natural selection for evolution among generations of humans (Cosmides and Tooby, 2000). Additionally, the principles of evolutionary psychology posit that psychological behaviours exhibited by individuals are determined subconsciously by an individual's neural circuitry with an individual being unaware of such subconscious processes. Reliance on conscious decision-making as a crucial guiding force in daily life is suitable for awareness of the resulting conclusions.

Nevertheless, individuals remain unaware of the underlying processes involved in such actions and decisions (Takeuchi et al, 2016). The principles of evolutionary psychology are closely linked to brain functionality as associated with the availability of neural circuits in the brain that are specialised to solve different adaptive problems. Additionally, the human mind is based on the adaptive changes as originally from the Pleistocene era.

At the most basic level of evolutionary psychology lays basic human skills, such as language, that are relatively simple and common to all humans. As man evolved, they developed skills beyond language and other basic skills. The ability of humans to communicate complex thoughts has been closely associated with human survival. Consequently, language acquisition skills evolved and advanced through natural selection. Advanced language skills are cited for human safety, reproduction, and survival.

Anterior Cingulate Cortex

The brain's function influences people's behaviours and decisions. In a study conducted by psychologists and presented in a journal, *NeuroImage*, it was established that brain activity varies based on individual thoughts concerning oneself. The research showed that brain activity reduced as the study subjects participated in competitions within groups compared to established competitions between individuals (Northoff et al, 2006). Consequently, it was evident from the research that people competing within groups were more likely to harm their competitors than those who did not exhibit decreased brain activity or acted as individuals in competitions. This study points out the changes in brain activity within groups. As such, it was established that groups were known for promoting anonymity, diminishing personal responsibility while encouraging individuals to reframe some harmful habits and actions as necessary for the greater good.

Research conducted by Cikara among a group of MIT psychologists started as a result of mob mentality associated with belongingness to an opposing sports team. This led to the decision by the graduate student to experiment on the neural mechanisms associated with group dynamics, consequently resulting in bad behaviour. In this study, the researchers conducted laboratory research that focused on the human brain's medial prefrontal cortex. When someone reflected on themselves, it was evident that this part of the brain would light up in the functional magnetic resonance (fMRI) brain scans. This experiment established that brain functionality differed when individuals played the experiments for themselves and when aspects of group moral statements were introduced. During team competition, researchers established that some people reported more negligible differences in group activity compared to individual activity, concluding that these were more likely to harm competing group members (Cikara et al, 2014). The neuro-imagery in this experiment was a crucial starting point in getting insights into some individual behaviours that had been complex to explain. Generally, it has been difficult for psychologists to understand people's behaviour as individuals and within group settings.

The brain's anterior cingulate cortex lies in a unique position within the human brain. It connects to the brain's emotional and cognitive aspects through the interconnectivity with the limbic system and the prefrontal cortex. ACC has a crucial role in integrating neuronal circuitry, thus affecting regulation and a crucial part of the brain in supporting a better understanding of psychopathology. The ability of individuals to manage and control uncomfortable emotions is the motivating force in various negative behaviours associated with nationalism.

The activities of the ACC are associated with decision-making, socially driven interactions, and empathy-related responses. Activation of the ACC part of the human brain has been considered crucial for error detection and outcome monitoring as crucial decision-making processes in humans. Consistent evidence exists regarding the crucial role of ACC in processing multi-modal context–related events compared to stimuli emanating from non-contextual events. Social cognition and interaction between individuals are associated with integrating flexible information related to the prevailing contexts (Takeuchi et al, 2016). This points out that the ACC could be a centre for the integration of information regarding the social backgrounds of individuals across various geographic and economic settings. Interaction between people belonging to the same group is likely to be totally different from interacting with individuals considered as belonging outside one's group.

Formation of Groups

Formation of groups along ethnic, racial, and national boundaries is key to the prejudice and treatment of out-groups. In his book *The Nature of Prejudice*, Allport considers the formation of groups as psychologically primary. This is based on the fact that attachment and familiarity for individuals within the same group come before the development of diverse attitudes towards the out-groups. In some cases, according to Allport, the preferential treatment of people within the same group and classification does not amount to negativity or hostility toward outsiders (de Carvalho, 1993). However, some cases of hatred, indifference, and disdain have been observed for a group of people against those who have been considered outsiders.

The concept of the over man, as introduced by Nietzche, points out the availability of groups surpassing individual identities. Here, the evidence suggests that the German philosopher was sceptical about individual identity and the notion of subjects regarding the behaviour and actions of individuals in society. According to Nietzsche, the elements of herd instinct and slave mentality could be used to explain and predict the likely behaviour of individuals and groups (Diethef, 1992). The herd instinct pointed to people's likelihood to blindly obey the masses without reflection. This idea did not sit well with the German philosopher, who sharply criticised the mentality. He felt that such a mentality was the primary cause of malaise in the civilisation. The concept made individuals follow blindly without questioning or thinking, thus being led like sheep in a herd.

Additionally, the spirit of equality was considered crucial in the herd instinct with people within the group required to be treated equally. Nietzsche held that people were and could never be equal to criticise this belief. He noted that hierarchy in societies could always exist with the strong dominating the weaker members of the society. Consequently, herd instinct was considered inevitable in society as it was challenging for an individual to adopt a moral value system outside of society. As construed by Nietzsche, the idea of an over man was to define a state of a human being having overcome themselves, thus gaining the ability to dominate those who have not. This pointed out the kind of leadership evolution in ancient societies and consequently, influenced community action and behaviours. The over man was considered an ideal theoretical construct designed to exhibit the difficulty of breaking free from society's ideological and moral grasp (Ansell-Pearson, 1994).

Ethnocentrism

Sumner also contributed significantly to the in-group formation and the resultant out-group treatment. He coined the concept of ethnocentrism in 1906, including the concepts of in-group and out-group. The term ethnocentrism itself refers to the tendency of individuals to remain ethnically centred and the rigidity associated with the acceptance of the culturally alike and the rejection of the unlike (Bizumic, 2014). Some examples of ethnocentrism in the past include the conduct of the ancient Greeks. This group believed that all other groups were barbarian while there was a distinguished group and sophisticated beyond the others in values, conduct, and behaviour. Aristotle also claimed that the Greeks possessed positive qualities that were adequately balanced compared to other groups at the time (Ward, 2002). This pointed out that other groups were somehow considered deficient in values and qualities considered common among the Greeks.

Hegel's statement about the Germans also pointed out people's prejudice against groups based on their presenting characteristics and features. According to Hegel, the Germans represented the objective spirit and could be seen as godlike (Hegel, 1999). The French also believed themselves to be more civilized than other groups of people in ancient times. The Chinese felt that their country was in the world's middle, while the Jews believed themselves to be chosen by God. Other ethnic groups had unique ethnocentric religious myths that placed them above other groups and people. The preceding discussion points out that each group has beliefs and customs that show them unique and superior to others.

Ethnocentrism empowers individuals to look at the world primarily from the perspective of their own culture. It is based on the belief that an individual's race, ethnicity, or cultural group is superior to others. While there could be some truth in such assumptions, no one group is superior to others in all aspects. Such an assumption is considered cultural ignorance and in most cases, has been considered a reason for strife between individuals from different groups.

Ethnocentrism leads to incorrect assumptions about the behaviours of others based on one's values, norms, and beliefs. In extreme cases, people categorised under one group may consider the cultures and norms of other groups as wrong or immoral (Brewer, 2001). In some instances, such beliefs have resulted in wars and cases of genocide as the superior group hates the members of other groups believed to be less superior and unimportant; thus, eliminating them is not considered a problem.

It would suffice to say that ethnic bias may be conscious or unconscious, resulting in forming a group considered a benchmark for all the other races and ethnic groups. This is considered a tunnel vision of reality based on the fact that different groups are likely to present different cultures, practices, norms, and behaviours. Such tunnel visions result in the inability of individuals to adequately understand cultures that are different from one's own. Additionally, individuals within groups considered superior may fail to value judgments that place other groups above others, thus linking the concept of ethnocentrism to elements of nationalism, racism, tribalism, and even sexism and discrimination of individuals based on their physical abilities.

Morality in Groups

Group morality revolves around the criteria defining acceptable and non-acceptable actions and behaviours in group settings. Morality shifts based on the presenting circumstances, and the aspects of the definition of norms change. Action according to the morally accepted principles allows individuals to be considered as part of a group or otherwise excluded as out-groups. Social psychology defines the concepts of moral feelings, behaviours, and thoughts as elements which individuals consider either right or wrong with a focus on individuals rather than groups (Leach, Bilali, and Pagliaro, 2015). While moral personality appears to have little influence on group behaviours, individuals' ideas regarding morality rely on some references regarding what are acceptable norms in society. Despite individual differences, elements of morality, or immorality are still reported within families, neighbourhoods, workplaces, and countries. This, therefore, shows that individual morality contributes significantly to the morality and behaviours within groups. Therefore, a sufficient understanding of groups and morality is crucial in understanding morality in general.

Morality is a central aspect of a group membership. Personality psychology determines how an individual see themselves and others in the manner through which they possess particular traits. The most prominent thoughts regarding moral personality revolve around the five-factor model:

openness and intellect, agreeableness, extraversion and conscientiousness, neuroticism, and emotional stability. Some of these factors touch on how individuals behave in communal circumstances through the possession of traits such as agreeableness and conscientiousness as well as personal traits such as openness, intellect, and extroversion. The socially shared conceptions of morality are crucial in anchoring people's internal moral compass and thus influencing behavioural choices among people living and working together. There is an increased motivation for people within the group to work together to maintain the status quo. This is exhibited in cases where in-group members may act immorally, calling for the defence of their actions by other members. An analysis of group behaviours showed that immorality within a group elicited threats to members those resulting in defensive action compared to instances of immorality by individuals outside one's group.

An assessment of morality shows that the concept is considered more of a social than an individual concept. Individuals confer in their moral values and considerations of morality based on the concept of self, yet morality cannot be purely considered as an individual item. If this were the case, it would be impossible for an individual to possess any sense of what others considered moral, thus influencing their decisions and behaviours while interacting with others. This means it would be impossible for researchers to imagine family, organisational, and group behaviours without considering some shared sense of morality. This has gone as far as considering an individual with a purely personal sense of morality as a psychopath who has personality disorders. According to psychiatry, psychopaths are individuals who fail to follow social norms and formal rules and laws. In other words, these individuals do not share common notions of morality in their groups. This indicates that morality is a socially shared convention implying the presence of a group in which members share, to some degree, the notion of what is considered moral or immoral (Cohen, Montoya, and Insko, 2006).

This does not, however, mean that morality can be considered perfectly consensual. Social sharing of the concepts of right and wrong does not eliminate the presence of individual differences or subgroup differences in actions and practices. Here, it is evident that morality is shared based on the fact that members have some common knowledge of an existing moral code used in the group however bad such thoughts are. Shared morality is vital for social relations among individuals considered part of a group.

All social interactions within groups allow for the existence of a common ground that allows parties involved to coordinate their behaviours (Carnes, Lickel, and Janoff-Bulman, 2015).

According to the philosopher Nietzsche, there we two kinds of morality among defined groups. The master-and-slave morality could be attributed to an individual's societal position. Master morality was considered to have originated from the noble and elite members of society, with slave morality originating from the weaker men (Nietzsche, 2004). These captured the different value systems existing in society and could be used to inform group action and behaviours in the face of various dynamic circumstances.

Master morality was mainly attributed to the strong will witnessed among those individuals who would consider and classify situations as good. The bad circumstances witnessed in society could be attributed to weakness, timidity, cowardice, and pettiness. Slave morality, on the other hand, originated from the weaker members of society. These are considered to be people who were uncertain of themselves and those who felt oppressed and abused in communal setups. In standard community setups, the influential members are fewer in number compared to their weaker counterparts. Consequently, this informed community behaviours as the weak regarded elements and qualities valued by the powerful in society as evil.

In-Group and Out-Group Dynamics

An in-group refers to a social group towards which an individual feels and shows loyalty and respect due to group belongingness. Loyalty towards one's group is characterised by in-group bias. On the other hand, an out-group refers to a social group to which an individual does not belong. Psychologically, individuals are likely to identify themselves according to their races, ethnic groups, cultures, religions, and gender. The psychological membership of social groups is a phenomenon in psychology that has been associated with various conduct and behaviour of groups resulting in in-depth research in the area to determine and inform structures and elements for group cohesion and coexistence (Abrams et al, 2003).

In-group favouritism is also referred to as in-group bias. It refers to the pattern through which individuals favour members of one's in-group over those that do not belong to an identified group. This is usually expressed in the manner in which resources are shared as well as the unfair evaluation of others. Research and experiments in psychology have shown that an individual is likely to award higher payoffs to people belonging to the same group, even though the criteria for such classification could be random and arbitrary (Fu et al, 2012). Two theories explain the relationship and treatment of individuals within and outside an identified group.

The realistic conflict theory states that conflict results in the fight for the same resources for a different group of people. As two or more groups fight for limited resources, there is an increasing likelihood of conflict, discrimination, and negative stereotypes and beliefs. Such conflicts will likely result in animosity towards outsiders and cause an ongoing feud between identified groups (Perry et al, 2018). An example of this theory is the conflict between the European countries Britain, France, and Germany due to competition for imperial colonies and power in Europe. To reduce conflicts between groups, researchers cite the creation of superordinate goals that bring more desirable results to the involved groups.

Social identity theory coined by Tajfel covers an individual's sense of who they are based on their group memberships. They proposed that the groups to which people belonged were an important source of pride and self-esteem. From this theory, the concept of us versus them arose due to social categorisation. Additionally, Tajfel introduced the concept of stereotyping based on normal cognitive processes, resulting in the likelihood for individuals to exaggerate the differences between groups and the similarities in the same group. The central hypothesis of the social identity theory is based on the fact that group members are likely to seek the negative aspects of those that do not belong to the same group in order to enhance the group's self-image (Tajfel and Turner, 2004).

According to the social identity theory, an individual's self-concept helps enable individuals to derive meaning about and evaluate themselves. Identification of individuals with specified groups helps members maintain a positive social identity, especially if the groups are highly sophisticated and rated superior. An individual's self-identity and esteem are tied to the experiences and perceptions of the groups to which one belongs. Any threats directed at a group may generate stress among group members calling on them to engage in different strategies to alleviate and reduce such threats.

Some aspects of intergroup bias while supporting a group to maintain a positive self-identity include in-group favouritism and out-group derogation.

This refers to discrimination of individuals based on their consideration as outsiders to a specific group. Such conduct is characterized by out-group hostility, negative evaluations of the out-group, and attributing negative traits and responsibility for negative occurrences to out-group members (Hewstone et al, 2002). Out-group derogation is not a frequent occurrence compared to in-group favouritism. However, it is considered a crucial concept to bolster and protect a group's social identity in the face of a group-based threat.

People are influenced differently by members within one's group. In cases where the categorisation of individuals is psychologically salient, there is an increased likelihood that people will shift their beliefs in line within-group social norms. Social influence covers the intentional or unintentional efforts at changing another person's beliefs, behaviour, or attitude. The nature of influence is non-goals directed with the outcomes more often than not likely to be linked with the communicator's goals. This is to say that individuals within an identified social group are likely to behave in a particular manner based on the accepted behaviours and norms in the group. In circumstances where a group member shows hatred towards the out-group, group members are likely to be influenced to follow suit. Social influence is characterised by strategies such as reciprocity, social proof, commitment, authority, scarcity, and attractiveness. Other crucial elements associated with social influence within groups include obedience, conformity, social loafing, social facilitation, peer pressure, and the bystander effect. In the long run, common conduct and action are likely to be observed among individuals categorised into one group. If hatred exists between one group and another, the same is likely to be perpetuated and followed through by members without reason and limitation.

Group polarisation is another crucial feature of an in-group and out-group dynamic. This refers to how the members of a group are likely to adopt extreme positions compared to members' initial attitudes and actions. This occurs because the collective involvement in groups amplifies individual attitudes and opinions and shifts them further toward group norms. Various theoretical perspectives were pursued to assess group polarisation's influences and the undying catering. Evidence suggests that polarised group decisions are made due to social decision rules, where individual decisions are transformed into group decisions. Informational influence is explained by how people learn from hearing and giving arguments regarding the topic at hand. Other critical influences for group polarisation include social comparison effects and responsibility dynamics, where a more significant number of people in a group may make others less responsible for any decisions and actions (Masuda and Fu, 2015). Choice shifts are also a crucial concern in group decision-making. Various perspectives have been put forth regarding the shift of choices, and the associated extreme group choices compared to those made by individual members within the group. The persuasive argument perspective posits that group polarisation occurs due to the content and arguments made available in decision-making. The group's purpose is to provide complete information to enable members to make more informed decisions.

On the other hand, the social comparison theory explores the fact that people within group discussions are likely to expose less extreme views than their actual thoughts for fear of being labelled deviant. When other individuals have similar or more extreme views, individual position shifts with a likelihood of the person exposing their actual values or even more extreme positions. As such, moderate positions are eroded while extreme perspectives are encouraged (Turner, Brown, and Tajfel, 1979).

The social categorisation theory, on the other hand, explains that group polarisation occurs when individuals within the group conform to an extreme norm or position put forth by a group. According to the proponents of this concept, group members are likely to modify their attitudes to fit the prototype position of the group in order to reduce the discrepancy between their initial positions and the implicit group norms (Turner, 2010).

The social decision scheme further posits that group decisions are linked to the initial distribution of attitudes and the decision role used by members to obtain decisions. Some group decision rules include majority role, mean initial attitudes, and extreme initial position, among others. Choice of decisions occurs when the decision-making rules generate group decisions that differ from the mean initial attitude of group members.

Psychologists describe the interdependency between group polarisation and choice shifts. While choice shift occurs due to the difference between the average attitude of the group members with the average initial attitude, group polarisation occurs when the choice shifts in the same direction and inclination as the initial average attitude of members. An analysis of in-group favouritism and out-group bias is explained here when members are likely to make an extreme decision on out-groups based on the initial views and feelings of members. Such decision-making has been associated with extreme conduct and aggressiveness against the out-group. There is the likelihood for group members to consider themselves more diverse and heterogeneous compared to those that belong to an out-group. These individuals and groups also consider and assume that the members of out-groups are similar to each other compared to the assumed diversity in the membership of one's group.

Unusual things are likely to happen when people categorize themselves into groups. Groups create social institutions enabling individuals to achieve objectives they could not have attained if they had been alone. However, the darker sides of such alliances touch on the fact that individuals are likely to hate those considered outsiders. Exacerbating this hatred could result in strife and even elements of civil unrest and wars, as witnessed in Rwanda during the genocide. It has been established that individuals who prefer equality and moral prohibitions cause harm in various contexts (Brambilla, Hewstone, and Colucci, 2013). This changes, however, following group formations and the classification of people into the us-versus-them classes. People will likely engage in actions against their moral standards, thus sweeping individuals into mob actions and attacks against other human beings. Individuals in groups are likely to feel more anonymous with a reduced sense of responsibility over collective actions. According to research by some psychologists, the concept that people were likely to lose touch with their morals and beliefs while acting in groups was raised. As such, they were likely to do things they would typically consider wrong.

Out-of-group morality is essential as it influences how people behave in general, as well as aspects of trustworthiness and perceived morality among people considered outsiders to one's group. Decisions by teams on whether to cooperate or compete with another group are based on aspects of trustworthiness. Consequently, a team's moral reputation is central to the group's decision to cooperate or compete with others.

Various aspects of the social world influence Moral judgment across societies and nations. Consequently, shifts and changes in moral accommodations witnessed during times of strife and violence are attributed to social agents' role in coordinating and configuring social networks. Social agents in societies play a crucial role in coordinating acceptable norms and morals and ensuring that individuals identified within a group comply with the acceptable way of life through such norms. In times of social strife within and among communities, it is highly likely that interested parties will recalibrate their determination of the moral standing of others, thus changing their perception of their established moral circles. Consequently, social coordination common in groups influences behaviour by inhibiting and promoting determining the individual ranking of moral priorities and the associated actions.

Group hate can be illustrated by the use of the disintegration of Yugoslavia along ethnic lines as a result of civil unrest in the 1990s. At that time, a majority of the country's population had held that their relationship with the neighbours resulted in a shift in ethnic sentiments resulting in the breakdown of the existing inert communal ties. As such, increasing instances of distrust between communities arose, resulting in violent outbursts between communities. While the first attack against the out-groups was initiated by insurgent military units, with time, attacks were witnessed among neighbours and friends and people who had known each other before. There was a significant shift in the fact that familiar community members were now considered enemies and were no longer accounted for as moral beings (Levin and Rabrenovic, 2001).

Morality can be used as a solution to complex issues facing communities and nations. The concept is applied in estimating the threats of competing interests on an individual's motivation and the need to maximise collective outcomes. While pursuing common goals, there is an increased likelihood for social agents to compete against others. Competition has been associated with instances in which mutual benefits are destroyed, resulting in conflicts likely exacerbating existing relationships across groups. It is only possible to advance expected benefits when individuals fail to address their self-interest. In communities and nations of efficient social order, forbearance is a virtue that keeps relationships going. It is a paradox since cooperation and coordination are crucial in managing conflicts and promoting safety and security. However, during such times, it is likely that groups are distrustful of each other. Leaders have often pursued moral emotions such as shame and guilt among various groups and communities to disincentivise vices. Adherence to established moral principles can encourage individuals to forego self-interest in favour of longer-term moral strategies.

References

Adorno, T W (2000) *The Psychological Technique of Martin Luther Thomas' Radio Addresses*. Stanford University Press.

Ansell-Pearson, K (1994) *An Introduction to Nietzsche as Political Thinker: The Perfect Nihilist*. Cambridge University Press.

Bairner, A (2001) *Sport, Nationalism, and Globalization: European and North American Perspectives*. Suny Press.

Bizumic, B (2014) 'Who coined the concept of ethnocentrism? A brief report'.

Brambilla, M, Hewstone, M, and Colucci, F P (2013) 'Enhancing moral virtues: Increased perceived outgroup morality as a mediator of intergroup contact effects', *Group Processes & Intergroup Relations*, 16(5), pp 648–657.

Brewer, M B (2001) 'Ingroup identification and intergroup conflict', *Social Identity, Intergroup Conflict, and Conflict Reduction*, 3, pp 17–41.

Brief, A P, Umphress, E E, Dietz, J, Burrows, J W, Butz, R M, and Scholten, L (2005) 'Community matters: Realistic group conflict theory and the impact of diversity', *Academy of Management Journal*, 48(5), pp 830–844.

Brock, G and Atkinson, Q D (2008) 'What can examining the psychology of nationalism tell us about our prospects for aiming at the cosmopolitan vision?', *Ethical Theory and Moral Practice*, 11(2), pp 165–179.

Burke, B L, Martens, A, and Faucher, E H (2010) 'Two decades of terror management theory: A meta-analysis of mortality salience research', *Personality and Social Psychology Review*, 14(2), pp 155–195.

Carnes, N C, Lickel, B, and Janoff-Bulman, R (2015) 'Shared perceptions: Morality is embedded in social contexts', *Personality and Social Psychology Bulletin*, 41(3), pp 351–362.

Cikara, M, Jenkins, A C, Dufour, N, and Saxe, R (2014) 'Reduced self-referential neural response during intergroup competition predicts competitor harm', *NeuroImage*, 96, pp 36–43. DOI: 10.1016/j.neuroimage.2014.03.080.

Cohen, T R, Montoya, R M, and Insko, C A (2006) 'Group morality and intergroup relations: Cross-cultural and experimental evidence', *Personality and Social Psychology Bulletin*, 32(11), pp 1559–1572.

Confer, J C, Easton, J A, Fleischman, D S, Goetz, C D, Lewis, D M, Perilloux, C, and Buss, D M (2010) 'Evolutionary psychology: Controversies, questions, prospects, and limitations', *American Psychologist*, 65(2), p 110.

Cosmides, L and Tooby, J (2000) 'Evolutionary psychology and the emotions', *Handbook of Emotions*, 2(2), pp 91–115.

de Carvalho, R J (1993) 'Gordon W. Allport on the nature of prejudice', *Psychological Reports*, 72(1), pp 299–308.

De Genova, N (2013) 'We are of the connections: Migration, methodological nationalism, and militant research', *Postcolonial Studies*, 16(3), pp 250–258.

De Schutter, H (2007) 'Nations beyond nationalism', *Inquiry*, 50(4), pp 378–394.

Diethef, C (1992) 'Nietzsche and nationalism', *History of European Ideas*, 14(2), pp 227–234.

Donnan, H and Wilson, T M (2021) *Borders: Frontiers of Identity, Nation and State*. Routledge.

Druckman, D (2001) 'Nationalism and war: A social-psychological perspective', *Peace, Conflict, and Violence: Peace Psychology for the 21st Century*, pp 49–65.

Dutton, E (2013) 'The Savanna-IQ interaction hypothesis: A critical examination of the comprehensive case presented in Kanazawa's The Intelligence Paradox', *Intelligence*, 41(5), pp 607–614.

Fromm, E (2013) *Psychoanalysis and Religion*. Open Road Media.

Fu, F, Tarnita, C E, Christakis, N A, Wang, L, Rand, D G, and Nowak, M A (2012) 'Evolution of in-group favoritism', *Scientific Reports*, 2(1), pp 1–6.

Gerlach, C (2010) *Extremely Violent Societies: Mass Violence in the Twentieth-Century World*. Cambridge University Press.

Goetze, D B and James, P (2004) 'Evolutionary psychology and the explanation of ethnic phenomena', *Evolutionary Psychology*, 2(1), 147470490400200120.

Greenberg, J, Pyszczynski, T, Solomon, S, Rosenblatt, A, Veeder, M, Kirkland, S, and Lyon, D (1990) 'Evidence for terror management theory II: The effects of mortality salience on reactions to those who threaten or bolster the cultural worldview', *Journal of Personality and Social Psychology*, 58(2), p 308.

Hegel, G W F (1999) *Hegel: Political Writings*. Cambridge University Press.

Hewstone, M, Rubin, M, and Willis, H (2002) 'Intergroup bias', *Annual Review of Psychology*, 53(1), pp 575–604.

Huszka, B (2013) *Secessionist Movements and Ethnic Conflict: Debate-Framing and Rhetoric in Independence Campaigns*. Routledge.

Islam, G (2014) 'Social identity theory', *Journal of Personality and Social Psychology*, 67, pp 741–763.

Jones, D (2018) 'Kin selection and ethnic group selection', *Evolution and Human Behavior*, 39(1), pp 9–18.

Kanazawa, S (2009) 'IQ and the values of nations', *Journal of Biosocial Science*, 41(4), pp 537–556.

Kećmanović, D (2003) 'The Psychology of Nationalism', Joshua Searle-White, New York, and Basingstoke: Palgrave, 2002.

Leach, C W, Bilali, R, and Pagliaro, S (2015) 'Groups and morality'.

Levin, J and Rabrenovic, G (2001) 'Hate crimes and ethnic conflict: An introduction', *American Behavioral Scientist*, 45(4), pp 574–587.

Masuda, N and Fu, F (2015) 'Evolutionary models of in-group favoritism', *F1000 Prime Reports*, 7.

McConvell, P (2010) 'The archaeo-linguistics of migration', *Migration History in World History*. Brill, pp 153–186.

McLeod, S (2007) 'Jean Piaget's theory of cognitive development'.

Nietzsche, F (2004) 'Master and Slave Morality', *Ethics*. Routledge, pp 173–177.

Northoff, G, Heinzel, A, De Greck, M, Bermpohl, F, Dobrowolny, H, and Panksepp, J (2006) 'Self-referential processing in our brain—a meta-analysis of imaging studies on the self', *Neuroimage*, 31(1), pp 440–457.

Perdue, C W, Dovidio, J F, Gurtman, M B, and Tyler, R B (1990) 'Us and them: Social categorization and the process of intergroup bias', *Journal of Personality and Social Psychology*, 59(3), p 475.

Perry, R, Priest, N, Paradies, Y, Barlow, F K, and Sibley, C G (2018) 'Barriers to multiculturalism: In-group favoritism and out-group hostility are independently associated with policy opposition', *Social Psychological and Personality Science*, 9(1), pp 89–98.

Smith, A D (2013) *Nationalism: Theory, Ideology, History*. John Wiley & Sons.

Staub, E (2012) 'The roots and prevention of genocide and related mass violence', *Zygon*, 47(4), pp 821–842.

Stewart, F, Holdstock, D, and Jarquin, A (2002) 'Root causes of violent conflict in developing countries Commentary: Conflict—from causes to prevention?' *BMJ*, 324(7333), pp 342–345.

Tajfel, H, and Turner, J C (2004) 'The social identity theory of intergroup behavior', *Political Psychology*. Psychology Press, pp. 276–293.

Takeuchi, H, Taki, Y, Sekiguchi, A, Nouchi, R, Kotozaki, Y, Nakagawa, S, . . . and Kawashima, R (2016) 'Differences in gray matter structure correlated to nationalism and patriotism', *Scientific Reports*, 6(1), pp 1–10.

Turner, J C (2010) 'Social categorization and the self-concept: a social cognitive theory of group behavior'.

Turner, J C, Brown, R J, and Tajfel, H (1979) 'Social comparison and group interest in ingroup favouritism', *European Journal of Social Psychology*, 9(2), pp 187–204.

Verdery, K (1993) 'Whither "nation" and "nationalism"?', *Daedalus*, 122(3), pp 37–46.

Ward, J K (2002) 'Ethnos in the Politics: Aristotle and race', *Philosophers on Race: Critical Essays*, pp 14–37.

White, F (1998) *The Overview Effect: Space Exploration and Human Evolution*. AIAA.

Williams, K P (2001) *Despite Nationalist Conflicts: Theory and Practice of Maintaining World Peace*. Greenwood Publishing Group.

CHAPTER 3

Introduction

Nationalism permeates various aspects of human life. To begin with, individuals are more likely to identify themselves with others based on various differentiating features. Such classification calls for the identification and adherence to specified group norms, failure to which one may be considered an outsider. At the same time, those who fail to conform to the commonly accepted norms and customs are shunned and considered outsiders. Consequently, conflicts could arise between various groups and divisions within and outside national boundaries resulting in armed conflicts or wars among nations. When such occur, the relationship between individuals and countries deteriorates as each conflicting party seeks to pursue its interest without considering the rights of its opponents. In such circumstances, it becomes difficult for people to coexist and cooperate on various national and international issues. The concept of international relations also features differing views and perspectives regarding national interest. How nations collaborate and coexist depends on each nation's diverse interests and goals. Where competition for scarce resources exists, nations are likely to engage in conflicts that could exacerbate the existing relationships and lead to fights between groups. Theories of international relations showcase various viewpoints and schools of thought to explain the different approaches to international relationships and the design and implementation of foreign policies.

The concept of national identity pervades societies, with children not being left behind by the various schools of thought. In an experiment to assess children's viewpoints regarding nationalism, it was established that children could classify people based on various differentiating features. Additionally, they could associate certain behaviours, actions, and characteristics with specified national groups. As they grew, however, the notion of national identity seemed to fade away as they understood that differentiating features were only attributed to the circumstances such as country of birth, race, or language as opposed to fixed and absolute features which individuals could influence.

Various researchers have delved into nationalism to determine its pathology while seeking to understand its impact on the peaceful coexistence of nations in the past. They have focused their efforts on assessing the factors influencing foreign policies among players in international relations. The outcomes showed the likelihood of people classifying themselves, with each of these groups pursuing their interests, thus affecting one group's relationship with the other. Some researchers noted that the classification of people along ethnicity, countries of origin, and national identity, in general, is baseless as such categorisation is tied to circumstances that place them together, such as common national origin.

National Identity

National identity is considered a crucial concept pivotal to the features reported in modern states. Classifying national identity concepts as exclusive and intolerant has contributed significantly to community persecution and aggression. On the other hand, national identity can be built around democratic and liberal political values and shared experiences of diverse communities. In this sense, national identity is crucial in enhancing physical security, inspiring good governance, fostering trust among citizens, promoting support for strong social safety nets, and making it possible for liberal democracy (McCrone and Bechhofer, 2015).

Perspectives on Nationalism among Children

Nationalist influences are evident in the lives of young children. Research conducted to assess children's perceptions of national identity established that they considered this aspect partly biological. According to the researchers, the roots of nationalistic sentiments across humanity could be attributed to thoughts and ideas obtained early in life. The researchers also noted that the biological perception of nationalism faded as individuals learned their history and those of others, thus diminishing this perception of nationalism.

According to Andrei Cimpian, an associate professor at the New York University department of psychology, as children grow, they perceive that their nationalism is a stable aspect of their identity. Although this deviates from the biological perspective evident in younger children, it informs the children's thinking process regarding whom they identify as beyond formal citizenship (Hussak and Cimpian, 2019). Through speculation, the psychologist suggests that the nationalistic sentiments among adults could be attributed to their thought processes and perceptions in their first decade of life.

The growth of globalisation, allowing for the free movement of people from one region to another, has not broken nationalistic ties even when the pressure associated with such moves is believed to influence how individuals feel about their origins. Despite changes in places of residence and work, it is evident that people still consider their national origins as a source of meaning for their lives (Søndergaard, 2003). In a survey conducted in America, more than 50% of the respondents cited their belongingness to America as either important or very important. Even individuals who immigrated from their nations of birth to other regions still feel attached to their home countries. They are likely to form associations with individuals from the same region as they share common interests, thus increasing the likelihood of coexisting without any struggles or adjustments (Ariely, 2012).

A rise in nationalistic ideologies has been witnessed in the twenty-first century. While researchers in the field believe that religion and sectarianism influence people's conduct in the twenty-first century, nationalism poses more influence as it wins in cases where the two are in opposition. Even in the Middle East, where uprisings have been thought to be religious, nationalistic ideologies have been used for or against one's enemies to their advantage or detriment.

The existence of national groups influences the relationships between people. In cases where strong national identification and belongingness exist, there is an increasing likelihood for people to show more negative attitudes towards those considered outsiders (Zhuojun and Hualing, 2014). In his campaign, while seeking votes as the president of the United States, Trump coined an ideology aimed at supporting US citizens, especially nationals, to restore their dignity as the country's citizens. Surprisingly, he received a significant following of individuals who felt they had more rights than others regarding access to resources and their overall stay in the country. Consequently, policies were passed that seemed to block or limit people considered outsiders from accessing full services compared to their native counterparts.

An analysis regarding the influence of national group concepts on how people view themselves on one side and others on the other informed the research conducted to understand human minds and how such concepts are represented. Cimpian and Hussak (2019) sought to assess such thoughts from childhood and whether such ideologies evolved as the children grew. The researchers carried out a series of experiments that covered children between the ages of five and eight years in America. The study aimed to compare the views of children versus those of adults. The participants were given questions/prompts to establish their views on factors associated with national identities. Given the nature of the study, the research sought to determine the feelings of children versus those of the selected adults concerning the connection between nationality, belongingness to a nation, and the biological aspects of human beings. Children were shown pictures of children from different nationalities and asked to answer whether the belongingness of the people represented in pictures would be linked to their biology. The participants were also asked about their views on the influence of a person's belongingness in other aspects of their lives regarding participation in sporting events and hobbies. The researchers also sought to determine whether children feel privileged based on their belongingness to America. In this case, there was a need to determine whether children believed that inequalities that gave them an advantage were fair and legitimate. The study's outcomes showed that children and adult participants felt belonging to a national group informed a person's preferences and behaviours. Additionally, such belief systems influenced aspects beyond the formalities of citizenship (NYU Web Communications, nd).

Husak followed up on the research to determine the meaningfulness of nationalism and its impact on the social world. He noted that nationality seemed to influence adults' concepts of national identity significantly, thus informing on the psychologically powerful nature of such thoughts even among adults. From the research conducted, differences were observed between adults and children. It was evident from the output that children connected national identity to physical and biological aspects of human lives and one with the capability of being passed down through generations. This was not the case for adult participants, indicating that such thoughts and perspectives on national identity diminished as children grew up.

Additionally, the study provided more insights regarding the impact of nationality in informing various aspects of behaviour and conduct among individuals. It was established that it was more likely that attitudes toward inequality and rationalization could be attributed to the beliefs held regarding one's origin (Charnysh, Lucas, and Singh, 2015). As such, participants of the study opined that an individual's nationality could inform a list of aspects regarding their day-to-day concepts. As such, they were likely to accept a status of inequality, especially if such favoured them.

Pathology of Nationalism

Nationalism arises from the concept of immigration, allowing for the movement of people from one place to another. Despite an individual's belief system regarding nationalism, the elements of immigration bring to light thoughts on borders, the creation of colourful multiethnic communities and exploitation of migrants on the one hand, and the impact of the arrival of foreigners that could affect the lives of aboriginals on the other hand (Janz, 2020). Despite an individual's political orientation, immigration brings thoughts on foreigners, states, and borders.

Methodological nationalism is a concept that seeks to explain the reaction of individuals to aspects of immigration and the movement of people from one region to another. The term expresses individuals' tendency to adopt nation-states' perspectives every time political questions arise (Chernilo, 2011). Here, individuals are likely to think that the world is divided into nation-states that define their lives. Additionally, these thoughts touch on the fact that individuals can be classified under a single state with cultures considered national.

Methodological nationalism, therefore, shapes how individuals view the world. Here, proponents of the concept agree that immigrants are considered foreigners while people living away from others are considered compatriots based on their national identity and origins. This is evident in the modern world, where people who have never lived in another state or country are considered immigrants just because their origin is not the current area of residents (Milioni, 2022). For example, an American citizen of Indian origin is still considered an Indian although his parents were born in America and themselves were also born here. Nevertheless, nationalists feel that such individuals should still be categorised as Indians!

Whether methodological nationalism is acceptable is based on an individual's perspective on nationalism concepts. Individuals who care deeply about national belonging and identities are likely to endorse the concept. At the same time, those who question nations' role in their lives are likely to oppose methodological nationalism (Wimmer and Schiller, 2002).

A critical aspect considered to be the undoing of methodological nationalism lies in its tendency to block our perspectives leading to the construction of certain identities. Consequently, this will conclude that such identities are natural rather than a matter of perspective. This leads to inflexible viewpoints hindering our ability to understand and communicate with others effectively. Under this perspective, migration is likely the movement of people across borders of nation-states (Wimmer and Schiller, 2002). Consequently, people who have remained within their nations would be considered sedentary as opposed to those who have moved from one nation-state to another as circumstances dictate. Even individuals moving within national borders would still be considered foreigners in their current areas of residence among foreign communities. Those moving from one region to another would still be required to learn their surroundings from scratch (Milioni, 2022). Failure to do so could result in conflicts between the aboriginal populations and the foreigners due to immigration.

Restrictions have been placed on migration based on understanding the nature of the nation-state. Here, it is considered natural for people to live within the confines of their nation-state and unnatural if they cross these borders. As such, the presence of immigrants is considered unnatural, disrupting a nation-state's self-evidence.

While studying the nature of nation-states, social phenomena are considered non-self-evident. Her actions and decisions are considered social reality. Thus, methodological nationalism highlights the tendency of individuals to lose sight of the nation-state perspectives seeing it as the truth governing the relationship between individuals within identified regions. In this perspective, there is an increasing tendency to understand the composition of nation-states as less ethnically homogenous communities with individuals sharing values and cultural norms. As such, actions and decisions within a nation-state will be taken based on this understanding

(Lazzeri, 2020). Consequently, migrants are expected to find their way into the homogeneity of the ethnic community within the nation-state.

Effects of Nationalism

Various commentators describe the adverse effect of nationalism in the European region. They note that the state of solidarity at the state level can become toxic, leading to isolation and intolerance when there is a need for cooperation in matters affecting humanity across the region (Van Evera,1994). One of the commentators describes the way of life of two different countries, Great Britain and Italy, and how the two pride themselves in their past. He notes that they have different national characters based on the factors that contributed to their creation with each expressing their pride through various markers and symbols. The writer of the article notes that even if he grew up based on social and generational influence in Great Britain, it was evident that his life was influenced more due to the common habits and concerns of people across the planet as opposed to the influence of fellow Italians. Some of the factors influencing identity, according to the author, include the influence of family, friends, cultural tribes, and any other influences as a result of close connection and proximity to an individual.

Other factors influencing an individual's identity include books, values, ideas, political dreams, social concerns, and common purposes shared, nurtured, and pursued in communities and across national boundaries. Instead of the influence of borders and boundaries on an individual's identity, it was evident that factors that influence an individual's conduct, behaviour, and way of life revolved around a combination of layers and intersections in layers of influences that weaved humanity together in the face of the ever-changing culture (van der Brug and Harteveld, 2021).

The writer questions why we build and organize ourselves along nations and their sense of belonging. Nevertheless, our own identities emerge from the kinds and levels of influences linked to those close to us. He concludes that such associations are based on the emergence of nationalism and national identities based on power structures. Instead of building power structures based on identities, it is the other way around. This indicates that identities result from power structures characteristic of the contemporary world (Lerner, 2022).

Any emerging power centre's influence promotes a robust sense of identity to divide people into groups. This is evident in the customization of the history of nations to focus on themselves rather than others that could have had a greater influence on the world order. For example, French history focused on the French revolution while Italians consider the renaissance with the Roman Empire a critical historical event. On the other hand, Americans appreciate the events that gave rise to the modern world as characterized by democracy and liberty: the war of independence. The article writer, therefore, notes that we live in a world full of discordant narratives fronted to explain our existence and tie us to certain identities. These narratives, unique among nations and those shared by their citizens, are designed to create a sense of belongingness to fictitious nations. Instead of fixed and never-changing influences of nationalism, it is evident that the concept is fluid, changing with the changing perspectives of leaders and those that influence the decisions in the nations (Gellner, 2008).

National identity politics proponents recognize this concept's critical role in unifying individuals living within the same region and acknowledging a common identity. They emphasise the importance of cooperation and collaboration between those that live together instead of the chaos that could arise if the same norms and values were not appreciated (Hill and Wilson, 2003). As such, individuals are more likely to benefit from cooperation instead of competition. Consequently, various authors note the crucial role of civilisation in promoting collaboration between individuals noting that things would have been much better if there were no borders. Bringing people together in a central political space is associated with benefits that accrue to all due to the prevailing peace and cooperation (Liu and Hilton, 2005). Reinforcing the peaceful coexistence among people with the same diverse cultural and national identities is crucial for keeping any irrational conflicts away, promoting the need for individuals to accommodate each other and work towards achieving common goals.

The toxicity of national identity arises from its benefits. What a paradox! A concept that could build cooperation and collaboration between nations, causing division and conflicts simultaneously? National identity may foster solidarity at one level while impending cooperation on a larger scale (Berezin, 2021). The invention of national identity in Italy was well-intentioned, with the founding fathers seeking to bring the Italians together based on common beliefs and norms. The concept, however, revolved into fascism with the extreme glorification of the Italian national identity (Geary, 2003). Fascism is centred on extreme forms of nationalism while opposing democracy and liberalism in nations. In these cases, rulers apply absolute power to suppress citizens' freedom, making all people subject to the powers of the state (Smith,1979). Fascism often employs violence to achieve the desired political ends, thus affecting the livelihoods of people within the nation. For fascist governments, using military powers against citizens has often been cited.

Consequently, this gave rise to Nazism in Germany. This is a fascist ideology that focuses on the state. Here, leaders gain the support of citizens by appealing to the people's sense of nationalism and racism, especially by promoting hatred and suspicion against people categorised as foreigners in a nation. From this state of affairs and its related consequences, it was evident that when people, especially leaders, valued conflict over cooperation while limiting the search for a compromise and agreed-on rules, thus making the concept of national identity toxic.

Many activities signify people's participation in fake nationalism. Participation in fake propaganda is such an example. An individual's opinion on certain issues and matters is crucial, yet the issue should lose its significance when it is not considered true as per the facts available. The tendency of individuals to share fake news, especially on social media while appearing to be patriotic is likely to create tensions and divisions among people resulting in unwanted outcomes (Kiper, Gwon, and Wilson, 2020). Some individuals blindly support specific political parties as a show of their patriotic nature. Such support towards a specified party without considering the related rational differences affects the relationship between one and others from different parties. Individuals must show support for a certain party while taking criticism from non-supporters. Religious-based nationalism is evidenced in how Christians are likely to dignify religion to the detriment of secular individuals within specified boundaries. There is a need for individuals to ensure that their honour is not associated with disrespect for others. Other aspects that have been closely linked to the fake show of nationalism among citizens across various national boundaries include maligning the image of founding fathers in nations, voting for criminals, underserving dynasties and religious fanatics, as well as certifying patriotism.

Nationalistic politics have been witnessed around the globe, leading to increased tension and conflicts and threatening the existence and livelihoods of individuals. Consequently, one writer feels that this concept should be declared fake. He notes that the concept of national identity should only be mentioned or applied to overcome narrow local interests. On the other hand, it should be left out and rejected if its aims at promoting the interests of single groups or nations above those of others for the greater common good (Rovelli, 2018)

Research shows that the concept of nationalism is tied to the policies of respective nations and their boundaries. The surge in nationalism and the concepts of localism in the contemporary world are associated with mistaken hopes for political gain, which draws on the emotional appeal associated with the insatiable need for individuals to belong to a specified group (Ishay, 1995). For politicians, the premise for offering homes for individuals based on their national identities is considered cheap and politically rewarding for the ruling classes. Thus, placing the concept of national identity beyond cooperation between nations and individuals is considered counterproductive, ugly, and morally irrational.

Often, as individuals put nations first above anything else, they are likely to betray others. This is so, especially among mixed-race nations. Betrayal is not associated with equality but with the existing difference between people within the same national boundaries. The writer argues the need for unity within diversity, resulting in the need for individuals to share values worldwide. Hostility towards immigrants witnessed the world over encourages xenophobia, affecting individuals' willingness to stay away from their homes and national origins. This also adversely affects human rights across various interest groups while upsetting the existing dynamics among nations, especially in the European Union (de Figueiredo, Elkins, 2003).

Another crucial factor in nationalism and national identity is how nations teach and pass on their history. In French, history focuses on the French revolution and the country's role in standing for its rights in the face of existing conflicts with humanity. Differences in these expressions of history based on the national identities of individuals are linked to discordant narratives that tend to raise others while stamping others under feet. These narratives have created a sense of belongingness and fictitious families where people are grouped, called nations. What is more confusing about nationalism and national identity is the dynamism of these boundaries created along the political arena.

One writer recognises the existence of boundaries in the form of nationalism yet notes that unifying people for the common good is wise politics. He also notes that fights among people classified based on their identities have negative implications compared to when people work together for the common good. He also notes that people can accrue more benefits by working together instead of competing based on national identities. Additionally, he argues that collaboration between people, despite their national identities, is associated with positive aspects of civilisation; hence, humanity could do better without borders Rovelli (2018). Researchers posit that humans are social. They can exchange goods, ideas, smiles, looks, and the stuff associated with the complex reality of human nature and the elements that make us richer in terms of intelligence, wealth, and soul. As such, bringing unity among people in terms of political space and ideologies is crucial for limiting and avoiding conflicts while creating awareness of the sacred nature of national identity.

Dangers of Nationalism

When people passionately invest in their own countries without consideration for others, some dangers could influence treatment and outcomes in relationships. The in and out-of-group thinking encourages division among people, often seen in sports as people support a team (Sapolsky, 2019). There is an increased likelihood that when a team wins, its supporters feel victorious even if they just watched the game without active participation. As such, they feel pleasure in others' defeat. According to Orwell, nationalists think solely about competitive prestige (Suddaby, Foster, and Trank, 2010). Nationalists are likely to think about defeats, victories, triumphs, and humiliations.

Nationalism pushes people towards a competitive mode. Individuals in various groups are committed to winning at all costs, characterised by power-seeking and superiority as factors influencing their thinking and actions. At times, nationalists feel justified in hurting others who are considered outsiders regarding national identities and origins. In the contemporary world, the will to power and selfishness are the determinate factors driving foreign policy design and implementation. These have taken over positive aspects and elements such as morality, long-term stability, and mutual benefit. These result in violence, broken agreements, indifference to the sufferings of others, as well as harm to countries and other people. It also increases the likelihood of destabilising global politics (Heller, 2011).

Another danger of nationalism is how it contributes to the fragmentation and instability within national boundaries. The concept requires individuals to decide on those who are part of the nation and those who are not. This contributes to exclusionary and prejudiced policies for individuals considered outsiders to a nation (Olzak, 2004). The marking of boundaries of a nation is bound to exclude others and affect their treatment and existence in the nation. The divisions among people within the same national boundary could be in the form of race, gender, and even their origin status, leading to perceived groups.

In cases where leaders are nationalists, they are likely to break the laws and fail to adhere to the constitution if such provides guidelines on the equal treatment of all people within its borders. When the constitution interferes with national ambition, such leaders are likely to set the constitution aside and depend on their understanding to make decisions and policies that could impact unity and peace within the nations. Such interference can be in the form of media control to report only aspects of national decisions and progress, interference with the judiciary, unlawful torture of individuals considered to be on the wrong side of the nationalist governments, and extrajudicial matters witnessed in some nations. Such leaders will likely influence organs of the government for their benefit and against those considered the nation's enemies, including the imprisonment of political rivals.

Another danger of nationalism is the tendency of leaders associated with this ideology to extort the truth for their benefit. Such leaders are likely to glorify themselves while distorting the truth to maintain the illusion of superiority. Here, they will likely pursue ways that make facts irrelevant while appealing to people's emotional well-being. Nationalist leaders are likely to resort to suppositions, fallacious reasoning, scorns, exaggerations, and inadmissible self-praise, as exhibited in the distortion of history. Consequently, historical facts are twisted into myths due to the fears linked to historical and social realism.

Nationalism and International Relations

International relations attempt to explain and explore the relationships between the interactions of states in the global, interstate system. Such exploration covers the behaviours and actions of people from one country and how much they treat others. In other words, the concept strives to explain the relationship of people across the state's boundaries and the existing governance structures that oversee and manage such interactions. However, explanations of human behaviour are complicated based on diverse perspectives, cultures, and the nature of the interaction between people. International relations touch on the psychological and socio-psychological understanding of policy decisions across national boundaries and the underlying factors for such decisions (Heiskanen, 2021). Another critical aspect of international relations lies in the institutional processes and political factors that contribute towards meeting diverse national goals while balancing the needs within a nation's borders and addressing outsiders' conflicting or diverse interests.

National interest is a critical concept in international relations theory. Nations are often engaged in the process of fulfilling and securing their interest. As such, the foreign interests of nations are derived from the need to address their national interests. This is considered a universally accepted right of nations to secure their interest. More often than not, states seek to justify their actions based on national interests. This covers aspects of a nation protecting its physical, political, and cultural identities against encroachment by other states or nations (Burchill, 2005). The term has often been termed ambiguous, carrying a meaning based on the context within which it is being used. Individuals, including leaders who make policies for their nations, often use this term to their advantage to meet their interests and to justify actions and behaviours. For example, Hitler justified expansionist policies to meet German national interests.

In contrast, US presidents have often justified the development and innovation of destructive weapons of war based on the need to meet America's security needs and interests (Rice, 2000). During the late 1970s and 1980s, the USSR justified its intervention in Afghanistan to meet Soviet national interests (Dimitrakis, 2012). Other examples of the use of national interest to justify actions and decisions of leaders and nations include the border disputes witnessed between China, India, and the Soviet Union as a means through which China sought to meet its national interests. In the contemporary world, P-5 countries are more likely to cite national interests to justify non-proliferation and arms control. Such ambiguity hinders the process through which nations can formulate universally acceptable policies.

The vital components of national interests, as expressed in the formulation of foreign policies, include physical, political, and cultural identity. Physical identity captures components of territorial identity. On the other hand, political identity touches on nations' political and economic systems. In contrast, cultural identity describes aspects of historical values that nations uphold as part of their cultural heritage. These components are crucial and are considered vital for the survival of nations. In cases where conflicts exist touching on these components, nations are likely to go to war or enter into conflicts to secure these interests. Nations often formulate foreign policies to secure and strengthen their security (Kratochwil, 1982). In the contemporary world, attempts to secure international security and peace are based on the fact that the security of the different states is linked to that of others. Thus, security is considered a vital component of national interest, with each nation more likely to secure it even through war.

Decision-maker perspectives, public opinion, the politics of leading parties, and sectional group interests determine non-vital components of national interest. These variable interests are the desires of individual states and which they will seek to achieve without necessarily going to war with others. These are often considered objectives of foreign policies. They could achieve prosperity within the nation, peace, attainment of identified ideologies and justice, prestige, aggrandisement, and power (Finnemore, 1996).

Thomas W Robinson defined various aspects of national interest to explain the relationship and decisions made in nations. The primary interests are those concerning which nations are unwilling to compromise. These cover aspects of preserving physical, political, and cultural identity against invasion and encroachment by other states. States and nations, therefore, seek to defend their primary interest at all costs (Robinson and Shambaugh,1995). Secondary interests are considered less important than primary interest yet is quite vital for the existence and continuity of the state. These cover aspects of citizen protection for those who are staying outside the country and promoting diplomatic relationships to ensure that the welfare of citizens is met. Permanent interests, on the other hand, refer to the long-term state interests subject to very slow changes. Variable interests are considered critical for the national good based on the circumstances. The diversity of personalities, sectorial interests, public opinion, political and moral folkways, and partisan politics influences these. General interest covers those that influence the condition of many nations in specified fields such as trade, diplomatic and economic relations to ensure that international peace prevails as a general interest of the affected nations. These also influence the desire of nations to pursue policies associated with arms control and disarmament efforts.

As nations seek peaceful coexistence with their neighbours, international interests take centre stage with the need to address identical, complementary, and conflicting interests. Identical interests are those that are common to a large number of states. Complementary interests may differ between nations yet form the basis for agreements among states on specific issues (Burchill, 2005). These interest groups are not absolute and may shift from one category to the other based on the circumstances.

Nations apply various strategies to secure their goals and objectives regarding their national interests. Diplomacy is a universally accepted method to secure national interest. Through diplomacy, the foreign policies of a nation can travel to others while a nation seeks to secure its goals and objectives. Additionally, diplomats seek to establish contacts with decision and policymakers in other countries by negotiating with them to achieve the desired goals and objectives regarding their nation's interests (Fendrick, 2012). Here, diplomas seek to design national interests, goals, and objectives to persuade others to accept them as just and rightful demands for a specified nation group. Persuasion and threats are the critical strategies diplomats use with rewards and threats of denial of rewards being used to exercise national power and secure goals associated with a nation's interests as defined in foreign policies. Consequently, nations apply diplomatic negotiations to resolve any conflicts between them.

In cases where nations' interests are not achieved through diplomacy, propaganda is applied. This is the art of salesmanship aimed at convincing others regarding the justness of goals and objectives of national interests that a nation seeks to achieve. Here, a nation seeks to impress others regarding the need and necessity to secure goals that a nation seeks to achieve. According to Frankel, propaganda is a systematic attempt to affect the minds, emotions, and actions of specified groups to achieve a specified public purpose (Jang, Hong, and Frederick, 2015).

Other nations, especially the rich and developed ones, apply economic aid and loans to secure their interest in international relations. The gap between the rich and the developing nations offers an opportunity for the rich to promote their interests against the needs of the poor. The dependence of developing countries on the rich ones for the importation of industrial goods, technological know-how, armaments, and the sale of raw materials is considered a critical factor in strengthening the role of economic instruments in foreign policies (Ahmed, 2020).

Other nations apply alliances and treaties to meet their objectives and goals. Here two or more nations come together to pursue and achieve common interests regarding identical and complementary interests. These alliances and treaties make it a legal obligation for established alliance members and signatories of treaties to work towards promoting their agreed common interests (Rubinstein,1999). Such alliances are often classified as either military or economic.

Coercion is another trait used by nations to pursue their interests. Power is considered an unwritten law in international intercourse, allowing nations to use force to secure their national interest. This could include war or exclude war, yet nations are forced to give in to the demands of the powerful nation in pursuance of their national interests. Some of the coercive techniques used by nations to achieve their interest include intervention, boycotts, embargoes, retorting, reprisals, and severance of relations (Lebow, 2007). A nation uses these approaches to force others to accept a particular course of action or to refrain from acting in a specific manner in order to serve the interests of others.

War and aggression have been considered illegal means of pursuing national interests. Nevertheless, other states and nations still apply this approach in order to achieve their goals and objectives with regard to achieving their national interests. Nations seek peaceful means of conflict resolution while pursuing their interests and needs. However, some are sometimes forced to use coercion when expedient and necessary with military power considered the major part of national power used by nations to secure their desired goals and objectives.

In the international arena, military power is considered acceptable as a natural and just means of fighting international terrorism. The world and public opinion accept the use of war as well as other forcible means to eliminate international terrorism, which is most of the times regarded as a means of nationalist states to force others into accepting their ideals and ideologies (Dumas,1990). Consequently, nations have the right to secure their national interests by using any acceptable strategies as mentioned above. As such, they have a right to choose any applicable approaches as may be available and suitable for them. Nations can therefore apply peaceful or coercive means to address their issues while seeking to push to achieve their goals and objectives in the long run.

In order to achieve international peace, nations are often advised to pursue peaceful means of settling any existing conflicts and limit the use of forceful means, especially war and aggression. While formulating their goals and objectives in the national interest, nations should pursue honest attempts to make them compatible with international interests, including peace, security, and protection of human rights, environmental protection, and sustainable development (Lake, 2007). Components of importance in international relations relate to peaceful coexistence, purposeful cooperation, and peaceful conflict resolution to attain nations' common and shared interests. As such, nations must seek to protect and promote common interests in the larger interests of the international community.

Realism Theory of International Relations

The concept of realism in international relations emphasizes its competitive and conflicting sides. Realism assumes that the nation–state is considered the principal actor in IR. While other bodies exist, including individuals and organisations, their powers are limited. Secondly, the state is considered a unitary actor with national interests, especially in conflicts leading the state to act and speak with one voice (Guzzini, 2013). Another assumption is that decision-makers are rational actors; thus, any decisions are made to support the state in attaining its national interests. Thus, decision-makers have to pursue actions and decisions to strengthen rather than weaken the state.

Realism claims that the world is a dangerous and harsh place with the only certainty attributed to power. This means that powerful nations can easily rule and influence others. Thus, they can outdo or outlast weaker competitors. As such, nations are in pursuit of military powers in order to showcase their powers and abilities over others. On the other hand, the state aims at self-preservation, thus pointing out the increasing need for states to seek power to protect themselves from harm (Crawford, 2005). Another crucial assumption in the realism theory is based on the fact that there are no overarching powers that can enforce global rules or punish any bad behaviours. As such, nations often pursue strategies that will preserve them while upholding their interests.

International morality defines how nations conduct themselves while making decisions that could affect other states. The moral codes

---

of conduct that govern the relationship between nations are crucial in attaining international legal order. According to the concept of realism, moral behaviour is considered risky as it undermines the ability of the state to protect itself. Consequently, the international system is thought to play a crucial role in pushing states towards the use of military force, thus degenerating into the use of war to solve any existing conflicts between them. While leaders may be moral, others fail to adopt and apply moral concerns in formulating and implementing foreign policies. It is vital to understand that international organizations exist to guide relationships and interaction between nations yet play insignificant roles in forcing nations towards adopting certain actions and decisions (Donnelly, 2000).

Realism and nationalism are considered *kissing cousins* in research conducted by Mearsheimer (2011). These two concepts are considered particularistic theories that assume that the key actors in the world are autonomous units that interact with each other based on circumstances. As interactions between nations could be harmful or helpful, these units pay careful attention to how their behaviour could influence and affect the outcomes of interactions. Each of these units commonly referred to as states or nations has the right to pursue its unique interests, even if such is done at the expense of other nations' interests. This has often led to conflicts, exacerbating the disagreements into wars. However, it is crucial to note that these units are not hostile to each other at all times (Lake, 2003). As such, they are not in a constant state of war. Nations and states sometimes cooperate in pursuit of common goals and interests.

The possibility of conflicts exists, and units have to stand by with the possibility that conflicts and misunderstandings could arise between nations. During such times, nations worry about their survival even if such threats may not become real. Among nations, survival is one of the priority factors. Even though it may not be the only one, it is the highest goal based on the need for the survival and continuity of states (Gleditsch, 2009). Accordingly, the state is considered the most powerful political institution in the world, with the same being the main unit of analysis in nationalism. Nations are considered political actors that must operate through specific political institutions to acquire and exercise power. In analyzing the concepts of realism and nationalism, nations are considered political actors that must operate through the political institutions put in place. Therefore, nations' existences are closely linked to the states; hence, the state forms the basic foundation for the states and the nation.

Realists assume that the states are the major actors on the world stage, bearing a significant impact on international politics. Additionally, states operate in anarchical systems without a central authority or arbiter that stands above any nations. Consequently, power is the main currency for international politics; nations compete with each other to attain and maintain power and authority over others. States are more likely to pay attention to the need for balancing power as they seek to gain power over others while ensuring that no other states shift the balance of power in their favour. In case of unjustified power shifts, realists are likely to opt for war as a legitimate tool for statecraft as linked to the ideology put forth by Clausewitz that war is considered an extension of politics by other means. Consequently, states face an ever-present danger of attacks by adversaries, and, in extreme circumstances, such enemies could threaten states' survival (Smith, 1990).

Different viewpoints exist among realists regarding the powers of states. Structural realists believe that states pursue power since they have limited choices regarding the need to access and maintain power. In a system where higher authority is available to control nations' behaviour, actions, and decisions and where there is no guarantee that one state will not attack another, each state is required and expected to protect itself in case of an attack. Here, states are left with little choice but to compete against each other for power as their hope for survival. According to structural realist theorists, power is the key survival tactic for states and, as such, overrides all the other objectives for their survival (Mearsheimer, 2007).

On the other hand, classical realists hold that states seek power based on human nature. Power is considered an end to this realist class. Morgenthau supports this theory, which holds that all individuals are born with the will to power being hardwired into them (Williams, 2004). This means that they are likely to pursue ways of dominating others. Additionally, the concept of survival seeps into this theory since states are considered to exist in a world characterised by aggression and the existence of potentially dangerous neighbours; hence states are always worried about their survival even if their ultimate goals lie in need to achieving more power for its own sake (Brown, 2009).

The Concept of Realism in International Relations

For realists, the international community is considered a device used by powerful nations to meet their interests. On the other hand, weak states appeal to international communities only to attain recourse from some of the issues facing them. As seen from real-world occurrences, international politics have often played out ruthlessly and dangerously, and it is likely to remain. Hence, different states/nations approach the international community with a focus on achieving their interests.

Realism touches on aspects of misperceptions among states. Its focus on this element is attributed to the fact that misperceptions in times of peace and war are so costly to both states and societies and could therefore trigger great interest affecting the ability of states to play international power games in the manner that they desire. Among strict structural realism, individuals treat states as security maximisers within a system where they are required to obtain a balance of power without adversely influencing the interests of others. Others within the same field consider states as power maximisers, characterised by their tendency to make the most out of the various aspects and factors in the international arena. Others propose that states seek to attain the balance between power and security as their main objectives in their national interest agenda. According to Mearsheimer (2007), states often face pressure towards forming an accurate representation of the world as characterised by their promptly responsive actions to others' powers. Accordingly, states seem to be deeply suspicious, seeking to assume worst-case scenarios in their interactions with others within the international arena while ensuring that they are well prepared in case the assumed situations arise. Even states that seek to maintain the status quo seem to be loss averse and are more likely to pursue expansionist policies that are likely to stifle the balance of power, thus counterbalancing other states.

Liberalist Theory of International Relations

Liberalist theory of international relations holds that the state is the principal actor on the world stage while acknowledging that there are no power, authority, and arbiters above such existing states. As such, these theorists assume that states operate in an anarchic system with liberal states considered peace-loving and good. Liberals are more likely than other groups to spread liberalism across the world with the ultimate aim of producing states that are liberal and accepting in nature. According to the liberal story, such states would be similar save for their sizes, as states are considered equal based on the concept of the sovereign equality of states. Such liberal states are part of a close-knit community of community states. The liberalism theory of international relations is universalistic. It is a transnational theory that looks into the coexistence of states and nations despite their differences as they all have common interests that could be pursued through collaboration and coordination of efforts between states (Mingst, McKibben, and Arreguin-Toft, 2018).

At the core of liberalism lies the need to respect individual rights. Unlike the realism and nationalism theory that emphasizes the state or nations, the liberalism theory emphasises individuals' critical role and existence. In this theory, all individuals, despite their identities, origin, and other classifying characteristics, are entitled to the same package of rights considered universal in their application. While a nationalist is likely to treat members of their group differently from those outside the group, the liberalist considers and accords the same rights to all individuals despite their groups and classifications. Liberals hold that human rights apply equally among individuals from all corners of the globe as characterised by a global community of liberal nations and states. As such, everyone deserves to be treated in the same manner as regards individual rights.

Sovereignty, a term strongly held by the nationalists and the realists, is a concept of less concern and emphasis for the liberals. According to the theory of liberalism, borders are soft and permeable as human rights transcend borders with people having common goals and objectives, and states have a right to intervene in the affairs of others that violate the rights of their citizens. This means that human rights are more crucial than the sovereignty of the states in a liberal world (Heiskanen, 2019).

Survival is not the main goal for states operating in a liberal world as the threat of war is not considered a crucial factor here. According to researchers and theorists of international relations, constitutional democratic societies do not go to war with one another. This is attributed to the fact that states in a liberal society rarely disagree on issues as the shared understanding of individual rights is common despite the existence of states and national boundaries. Nations in a liberal society consider themselves as part of a larger community. As such, states have benign intentions towards each other with this factor widely acceptable across states. When disagreements arise between states, as this is common in cases where boundaries exist with states having different goals and objectives, liberal states seek to address such issues peacefully and do not indulge in war. Here, the focus is on international law, institutions, and acceptable conflict resolution strategies, not on the balance of power between states. Liberalists' masses are optimistic based on the assumption that states can overcome any existing constraints and limitations by cooperating to solve any existing security dilemmas through the pursuance of collective action and creating an open and stable system for the continued existence and sustainability of states.

Classical liberalists and conservatives believe that war is a necessary evil at times, yet engaging in it should be only considered as the last option. Nations can therefore engage with others around the globe through more meaningful strategies such as trade and diplomacy. Additionally, these groups acknowledge that military powers may not be suitable for solving every foreign policy problem that nations face from time to time (Halper and Clarke, 2004). War is also costly to nations based on the need to centralize executive powers for coordinated decision-making, affecting the civil liberties of a country's population.

Marxist Theory of International Relations

Marxism theory of international relations offers a universalistic perspective in international politics. Here, the main focus of analysis lies in class analysis which is far superior and more important than national groups and state borders. According to the Marxist theory, a powerful bond exists between individuals within the same class as opposed to a focus on the nation's identities. Given the transnational nature of classes in Marxism, the states fail to attract solid attention compared to its emphasis on realism and nationalistic theories of existence among nations. In this theory, the states are predicted to fade as the society transforms into a classless society where the rights of all individuals are taken into account despite their differentiating characteristics. The states are critically important concepts in cases where capitalist classes are influential. As such, states are likely to engage in violent conflicts to retain their power and influence over others and maintain their survival in the dynamics existing in contemporary societies (Lacher, 2016). As the proletariat gains final victory in the theory, class conflicts are eliminated as the political conflicts attributed to the different classes are eliminated, reducing the need for the existence of states. This results in the attainment of the Marxist objectives where different classes support each other for the achievement of common goals. Here, survival is not a major concern with the theory telling the optimistic story of the progress in human development and evolution.

Creation of the States System

Politics are attributed to the creation of the state system in the world. Before the emergence of nations/states, the various political entities in the European region engaged in ongoing security competition sometimes exacerbated into wars. As the states emerged in Europe in the fifteenth century, they had little choice but to worry about their continuity and survival as the threat of being wiped out of their existence always persisted. States had to use military strategies to stay alive in a dangerous world where only powerful actors seemed to survive. During such times, states were considered superior based on their ability to form military powers and win wars (Crawford and Crawford, 2006). Military capabilities at the time depended on the states having money to finance their armies and military, as well as the existence of a large number of people to build large fighting forces. States, more often than not, had to attract resources from their population hence the need to have a larger population for higher and superior fighting chances and survival capabilities of nations.

The survival of individuals/groups at the time depended on states, as cited by Machiavelli in the *Prince* (Machiavelli, 2004). At that time, the Italian peninsula was dominated by small city-states fighting each other to gain dominance in the region. Divisions were considered detrimental to the existence of the nations. He noted that as enemies approached, such existing divisions were likely to lead to the loss of cities as the weaker parties were likely to join the external forces reducing the ability of the others to rule. According to Machiavelli, the optimal solution to solving the problem lay in creating single states as exhibited in the push for the creation of Italian states that could stand against the neighbouring states and ensure the survival of the Italian state. The emergence of nationalism among the French affected the surrounding nations. The concept resulted in the powerful allegiance of the French people to their government as exhibited in their willingness to fight and die for the nation. This was a multiplier force that resulted in the Napoleonic and revolutionary French creating a powerful mass army to fight for the rights of the nation/state.

Following the French revolution, various surrounding nations felt the need to imitate the French by forming nations/states to fight for their survival and the achievement of their national interests. Such evolution in the existence of nations resulted in the formation of nation-states across the various borders in the European region by the early twentieth century. Sovereignty was the pillar of the existence of nations, coupled with power politics and the emphasis on the survival of nations (Keitner, 2012). Evolution in the existence of states resulted in the increasing need for nations to create their states. This was considered the best way for them to maximise their prospects for survival in a world characterised by competition. Various researchers in the area supported the proposition for nations to have their states as this could ensure a wide degree of national autonomy characterised by a range of possibilities for individuals within the nation to enjoy national life.

Concerns regarding the survival of nations have been associated with a host of factors. The intrusive nature of modern states has been one of the significant factors influencing how they carry out their duties and operations to protect them while ensuring their continuity (Biersteker, 2013). In the past, the dynastic states did not interfere in people's daily lives within their borders. Its primary role was the collection of taxes as well as the engagement of young men who could serve in its armies. Apart from that, people were left to operate within their own cultures, norms, and way of life. In the nineteenth century, the situation changed drastically as the state became more deeply involved in the lives of its citizens.

Consequently, states started adopting powerful incentives aimed at homogenising the people inside its borders into a single culture, shared history, and the use of a common language. At that time, this made sense as the leaders looked at the economic efficiency associated with the homogeneity in workers as supported by the creation of education and training guidelines to support knowledge creation and skill development among workers. Research following the need for uniformity among people within borders showed that educated soldiers were more efficient than their illiterate counterparts. Consequently, soldiers that spoke the same language and shared the same customs would be integrated into a better fighting force in a bid to protect the interests of the nation/state. It, therefore, made sound economic and military sense to have a well-educated population sharing a common culture as leaders established states to guide their interests.

The impulse to bring uniformity among people living within specified physical territories and borders became the beginning of conflicts and disagreements among people within and outside a nation's borders. These actions and decisions posed a great danger, especially for the minority groups whose rights were disregarded in favour of the majority interests. The majority in multi-national states were more likely to control the assimilation process supporting the adoption of its culture, language, and other cultural norms as the universally accepted way of life. Minority cultures were likely to be pushed aside with some disappearing. Walker Connor (1993) noted that while states sought to engage in activities associated with nation-building, they were also in the business of breaking the nations. This called for the push towards establishing states as per national boundaries resulting in the breaking of multi-national states over the past two centuries.

Another critical concern for states' survival lies in danger associated with conflicts exacerbating into a war that could wipe out their existence. An example of such an occurrence is the Rwandan genocide, which deteriorated into severe loss of lives and property as the murderous campaigns of two major tribes in the region deteriorated into war. Here, the murderous campaigns were driven by many reasons that could include resentment of the minority by the majority group as a result of the need to control the nation's economy (Pottier, 2002). To avoid such occurrences, nations sought to create their states to ensure that people within specified national boundaries were homogenous, sharing the same beliefs, cultures, and ways of life.

Nationalism and Conflicts

The concept of nationalism is witnessed in cases where rather benign nationalism has turned into hyper-nationalism resulting in resolution into wars as nationalists believe that inferior groups should be dealt with severely, leading to wars and ongoing conflicts (Kaufmann, 1996). When nations place great value on their unique cultural identities, they are likely to control their political fates. They are likely to pursue self-determination, characterised by the need to participate in political processes. As such, nations seek to get their states even though this is not achievable in the real world.

Nations are justified to worry about their survival and continuity, especially in a world characterised by the threat from other nations and the commonplace existence of hyper-nationalism. Nations also care about their survival when they do not have their nation-states as there is the possibility that more powerful nations may attack them, threatening their existence and continuity.

Armed Conflicts

Armed conflicts within states are often attributed to political conflicts that involve citizens and are often characterised by the classification of people based on identities and other classifying features. Such fights seek to achieve internal change within nations and states, resulting in the loss of lives and property. Some of these armed conflicts are categorised as secessionist movements spearheaded by people often considered minorities in states who take arms to fight to establish an autonomous entity to take care of their needs. Other cases of armed conflicts in societies revolve around the need for people to seize the powers of the government to meet their selfish interests (Moir, 2002). In some cases, such conflicts have even been categorised as organised crimes as opposed to the need for individuals to achieve their political will and desires. For such groups, money and power is their objective. Such groups do not wish to cease being members of a state. Instead, they would wish to continue living in the same territory with other existing groups despite the outcomes of such conflicts.

Some of the armed conflicts are fought by organised armies. In contrast, others are fought by militias and armed civilians with a small amount of discipline and inadequate chains of command, leading to the loss of lives and property with less accountability on the part of the fighting groups. Such conflicts, especially within states, result in the loss of critical institutions such as the judiciary and the police, which would have played a crucial role in conflict resolution and management, thus exacerbating the situation (Jentzsch, Kalyvas, and Schubiger, 2015). Such occurrences result in governance paralysis, the breakdown of law and order, general banditry, and chaos in societies. In some cases, government functions are suspended, leading to the destruction of property and looting with several people losing their lives. Here fighting can be considered intermittent based on the range of intensity and the fact that it occurs among communities as characterised by acts of violence and atrocities committed against others. In worst circumstances, this deteriorates into genocides wiping out communities from the face of the earth.

In the twentieth century, armed conflicts took an upward trajectory as communities and states sought to attain their national interests without due regard and concern for the needs of others, including their neighbours and minority groups within them. It is evident from research that such wars result in mass casualties of civilians, which is attributed to the fact that such wars are primarily fought within states and not between them. Here, villages and streets have become battlefields with traditional sanctuaries and hospitals being considered targets, which in part could have provided refuge to the victims of war. Armed conflicts destroy crops, schools, and even places of worship with nothing being spared. Additionally, more and more civilians are involved resulting in bloodbaths since small and light weapons are readily available (Levy and Sidel, 2016).

The worst-case scenario among fighting communities is the involvement of young children in the defence of one's nation or state. They are used as soldiers, especially during prolonged periods of civil wars. Reasons cited for children's engagement in armed wars include that they are docile, less likely to complain, and easily modulated to fight ruthlessly. Additionally, they can carry lightweight and high-powered weapons. Most of these young combats are also not afraid to die compared to their old counterparts concerned about their livelihoods and those of their families during wars. The young men, on the other hand, have nothing to lose and are willing to sacrifice their all for their countries (Kadir et al, 2018).

Wars within states/nations are caused by the existence of ethnic and religious animosities as well as the mass violation of human and minority rights leading to the ethnic cleansing that results from extreme forms of nationalism propagated by hate media. Another crucial factor is the rate at which arms are trafficked globally, especially in regions affected by armed conflicts. This makes it possible for the warring parties to access weapons with which they defend their interests at whatever costs without concern and regard for the needs and rights of its people.

Nationalism has also fuelled the control of natural resources and endowments for nations. This, coupled with broader political ambitions, has seen countries and states engage in civil and national conflicts leading to the likelihood for the winner to control a significant share of such resources (De Cleen, 2017). Access to such scarce resources is closely linked to the power with which nations rule and control others.

Armed conflicts significantly impact civilians compared to wars between states as the war combatants have increasingly targeted civilians in their fights. This is more likely to force the other warring party to concede defeat to protect its civilians. If that does not happen, those more civilians will likely lose their lives, property, and source of livelihood. Societies ravaged by such armed conflicts have paid heavily in terms of massive loss of life and political, economic, and social disintegrations resulting from such occurrences. Women and children have specifically paid an enormous price for armed wars. They make the majority of those who are killed and violated. These special interest groups have often been seriously injured or permanently disabled. Many have been injured due to landmine explosions, and others have been psychologically scarred by the violence resulting from such conflicts (McKay,1998). Some have been forced to take part in horrifying acts of violence with commonplace insecurity and trauma associated with civilian suffering due to such wars.

Instances of conflicts have been witnessed even as nation-states seek to remain powerful compared to their counterparts or competitors. The leaders of nation-states push for the establishment of robust systems to support their survival in the rough and tumble of international politics (Lerner, 2020). The power of the state is achieved through the establishment of systems to protect them while at the same time protecting the nations that underpin them. Such realist logic motivates the existence of power politics while influencing nationalism in various ways based on the presenting circumstances.

Nationalism influences international politics based on its contribution and pushes for the balance of power among nations. The concept of nationalism pushes nations to build large and powerful armies to protect their borders in conflicts and disagreements among states. The distribution of power among states, therefore, influences the way of lives of people and determines which among the states are likely to win or lose in case of war.

Nationalism is crucial in creating tight bonds among people living within specified boundaries. It would therefore be more manageable for leaders to call on their citizens to participate in the military and provide the government with a steady flow of resources to defend its boundaries. People are willing to make great sacrifices for the sake of their governments, as witnessed in their willingness to fight for the interests of the government despite the dangers of death, disability, and loss of property lurking behind such occurrences. Nation-states are therefore considered powerful enough to raise large militaries and sustain them for extended periods even if such occurrences are detrimental to the people and the government. This is evident from the fact that people across nations joined their countries' military in the world wars reported even if the dangers associated with such move were too grave to bear. As soldiers lost their lives, others joined in to fight for their governments' interests and well-being, exacerbating the war's severe consequences for all the nations involved.

Following the introduction of nationalism in states, the people's loyalty changed, resulting in soldiers, airmen, and sailors who were more willing to sacrifice their lives for the states than people's behaviour in dynastic societies. In these settings, there were low levels of loyalty, as seen in the desertion witnessed as most people who were, in most cases, just mercenaries left the army to protect their lives and property. As nationalism took centre stage among nations, the problem of desertion became less of an issue as the fighting forces were now willing to put themselves in harm's way to protect and defend their countries. Napoleon declared that all men who valued their lives and property more than the need to defend their nation and their comrades' esteem should not be considered part of the French army (Paret,1993).

Nationalism bears a critical influence on the outcomes of war among conflicting nations. The effect is significantly felt when one side of the competing or fighting nations uses a powerful military and applies brutal force against its opponents. In contrast, the opposing side lacks or does not invest massive resources in developing and training its military capabilities. An example is a French army that applied nationalistic concepts in the wake of its revolution creating the most powerful army feared by most nations in the European region.

The war between Israel and Arab rivals also showcased the crucial role and impact of nationalism on war outcomes. The conflict involved the civil war between the Palestinians and the Zionists in 1948 and the international war between Israel and five Arab armies (Schulze, 2013). In the first part of the war, the Jews were outnumbered by the Palestinian army, yet the Zionists were far superior to their counterparts, influencing the war's outcome. The Zionists thus defeated the Palestinians in the first half of 1948. In the second fight with the five Arab nations, the Israeli's army was much larger than the five nations combined. The war's success for the Israeli army can be attributed to their commitment to nationalism, their determination to create a Jewish nation, and the willingness of the soldiers and the people, in general, to make enormous sacrifices for the state. Zionist leaders worked to establish institutions that would be crucial in establishing the Jewish state, thus fostering greater nationalism among the public.

In the Arab world, on the other hand, nationalism was considered a weaker force beginning to be acknowledged at the time. There was little connection between the states and their people, thus hindering the ability of the Arabs to raise efficient and large military forces to counter the attacks of the Jews. The defeat of the Palestinians is linked to the little sense of nationhood as well as the lack of any affiliated institutions. The five Arab states, with a less developed sense of nationalism, faced bottlenecks in extracting resources from their people and generating strong military forces. Israel was bound to win the war based on its preparedness and the fact that its people and military were well prepared to defend the country against any attacks and defeat by the Arab army (Dawisha, 2016). Consequently, this showed that nationalism could be a considerable force with the potential to shift the balance of power, thus affecting the winners and losers among warring parties.

Nationalism has been cited as having an effect on how wars are fought as well as the form they are likely to take. In modern nation-states, wars are likely to take a final form where each of the parties fights to attain its goals and meet its national interests without compromising with the other warring party. Each of the war parties is less likely to accept nothing less than a decisive victory over its enemies. In such circumstances, it is difficult for the warring teams to fight wars with limited force and aims. This is evident in the fact that wars were occurring in the European region before nationalism was considered limited in means and scope.

Modern wars are likely to escalate into total wars because national armies tend to be significant with sufficient substantial powers to persist in their fight, thus their suitability for waging war against their opponents. When large armies are involved in the fight, violence, hatred, and enmity are high. This kind of hostility results in the resolve by the armies to pursue their interests without limitation to settle for less. Additionally, the concept of nationalism in countries pushes governments to motivate their public to make great sacrifices for them to win the wars. Consequently, a substantial mass of the population has to be convinced by the government to serve in the military and possibly die in support of the country. Here, people are motivated toward fighting their adversaries because the government paints them as an evil that seeks to break a united nation or state. This makes it difficult for the nations involved in the wars to negotiate and arrive at a suitable position as the army and leaders are not willing to compromise on their stance and the objective of the ongoing war (Crusher, 2021).

Nationalism causes war and disagreements between nations based on the hard stance that it gives governments regarding their need to achieve their interests before considering those of other nations. In some circumstances, the political arrangements of different nations are likely to cause intense hostility, which could escalate to war among countries. In some circumstances, nationalism makes war more likely to occur between two nations. First, nations without their own states are more likely to feel threatened by other national groups and would be willing to fight to gain their own states (Gibler, 2012). This was evident during colonisation as countries fought to gain their independence and enjoy self-determination from their colonisers.

In the same way, minority groups are likely to fight to break free from the majority and dominant groups that often seek to dominate them and fail to recognise their unique needs within established national boundaries. As a result of nationalism, states are also likely to go to war to acquire territory that contains fellow nationals. This is evident in the ongoing war between Russia and Ukraine, as the Russians feel that part of the Ukrainian territory is rightfully theirs D'Anieri, 1997). This has resulted in untold suffering for both parties as exhibited in the loss of lives and property for the two nations involved.

Nationalism is considered a crucial factor in the relationship between nations in the contemporary world. The ideology poses a challenge to international stability as well as regional global order. It encourages a narrow definition of security policies by opposing compromise and consensus among nations while undermining international cooperation and trust. Thus, nationalistic movements and states pose severe challenges to existing states and international order. On the other hand, nationalism is cited for contributing to the development and stability of international order. Researchers are left to wonder how nationalism will likely affect the future of international cooperation and multilateralism.

Various researchers have conducted in-depth studies on the impact of nationalism on the relationship between nations in history and contemporary societies. They note that the existing nationalist discourses that favour domestic unity have often led to the design and implementation of careless foreign policies, adversely affecting the relationship between nations and creating international conflicts. According to Posen (1993), nationalism is cited as having contributed immensely to the intensity of war by increasing the capacity of states to mobilize and bring together energies vital for war and promoting the spirit of self-sacrifice among individuals within identified national borders. Another researcher, Schrock-Jacobson (2012), identified various effects of nationalism on international relations. He noted that nationalism supported the identification of individuals according to their perceived groups of belongingness.

Consequently, this led to the defamation of these individuals, perceived as outsiders to the specified national boundaries. Such classification, identification, and defamation of others could be the fire necessary to fuel conflicts and wars across international levels. The defamed societies, communities, or nations are likely to react violently, leading to war and prolonged conflicts among nations that had previously been considered friendly.

Another crucial contribution of nationalism to international conflicts and associations between nations is the likelihood of nationalist states adopting biased strategic assumptions. Just like decision-making in companies, nations also adopt various strategies that influence their relationships and interactions with others. Biases in such processes are likely to impact the relationship between countries adversely and could lead to conflicts and wars. It is highly likely that in strategic formulation, areas of disagreement outnumber the areas of agreement. Strategic business problems have been labelled as unstructured and messy, just like any strategic biases in international relations matters. Such affects the nation's state and its relationships with neighbours and other international players, thus calling for a more careful approach in formulating strategies to lead a nation and influence its interactions with others.

Other effects of nationalism on international relations relate to the fact that some domestic interest groups could easily take advantage of established nationalist foreign policies by using them to lobby for the continuation and escalation of issues. Such occurrences result in conflicts between nations which are likely to escalate to wars if not handled in time. Another crucial impact lies in the likelihood of elites marginalizing opposition groups by describing them as national threats (Brown,1998). Here, adverse actions and decisions are likely to be made by nationalist leaders against forces that seem to oppose their behaviours and decisions. Additionally, nationalism is cited as a crucial element creating a favourable environment for nationalist wars between elites and those classified as elites against the masses who form the majority in any classification and division of individuals into groups in any identified national boundaries. Any nationalist processes, therefore, increase the likelihood of interstate conflicts, which are likely to escalate if decisive actions are not initiated to avoid such.

Peace in International Relations—Theories

International relations theories seek to explain past state behaviour and predict states' expected behaviours for the future. Traditional international relations theorists focus on the role of humans, states, and state systems in conflicts.

Scholars in the international relations field have pursued research into the various strategies that could be applicable in restoring peace among warring states and nations. Critical among them is the bargaining process theory. The main objective of the bargaining theory is to resolve international conflicts peacefully through negotiations. The bargaining process differs based on the parties involved and their different goals in the conflict resolution process. In the orthodox bargaining process, negotiations are made between the warring parties with the negotiating parties required to constantly hold their demands and objectives regarding achieving peaceful coexistence (Powell, 2002). Here, the preference schedules of the negotiating parties are required to remain constant. It would be irrational for the negotiating parties to keep changing their demands and preferences in the negotiation process.

On the other hand, the change negotiation approval developed by Burns in his book *The Prospects for a General Theory of International Relations* (1961) acknowledges that the conflicting parties' demands are likely to change in the negotiation. The approach, therefore, seeks to provide guidelines on managing such changes to ensure that the conflicting parties arrive at the most convenient outcomes for peace to reign. On the other hand, the theory of quasi-negotiation acknowledges that in specific negotiations, no party wishes to reach an agreement. On the other hand, such parties want to avoid considering the prospects of being considered failures due to failed negotiations between two nations. Additionally, no party would want to show their reluctance towards attaining peaceful negotiations and coexistence. Such parties propose unacceptable elements in their demands to the other negotiating parties, thus leading to the rejection of the demand and the parties' achievement of their negotiation objectives.

Status signalling in international politics is another crucial strategy for addressing existing conflicts between nations/states. It refers to the application of a specific subset of signals aimed at conveying information that a state seeks to assert an individual standing in the international community. It is the mechanism through which information is transmitted regarding the need to change or maintain a specific status belief among different political actors in the international arena (Morrow, 1999). Since the audience differs in their interest and objectives in the international scene, the emerging power sends a mixed status signal as a nation seeks to specify its standing. Consequently, nations apply mixed signals strategies to declare their position regarding an ongoing conflict to gain a peaceful coexistence among nations.

Social-Psychological Understanding of International Conflicts

A socio-psychological perspective on international relations is crucial in exploring the factors that affect the rationality of a nation to attain peaceful coexistence and cooperation. The approach seeks to explain the state as a unitary actor while analysing the processes in societies that influence states' actions and broadening the range of influences that affect international politics. Additionally, the approach seeks to define conflicts in the international arena as dynamic processes influenced by the changing realities, interests, and relationships between conflicting parties. The social-psychological approach provides a deeper understanding of conflict progression with the setting in motion of powerful forces that escalate and perpetuate conflicts between parties (Taylor and Moghaddam,1994).

Some factors that influence conflict in international relations include the formation of collective moods. This is characterised by the shift in public opinion regarding the issues that bring conflicts between nations or states. At various times, the moods of the conflicting parties could be optimistic, pessimistic, angry, defiant, and conciliatory, among others. Such moods affect conflict progression and influence the outcomes as conflicting parties seek to address the underlying issues (Stein, 2013).

Another crucial factor cited as having perpetuated conflicts in international relations lies with the mobilization of group loyalties. As leaders arose feelings of nationalism and patriotism among citizens, people were likely to take sides. As such, they offer support to leaders, which could further fuel the conflicts between parties and influence the overall outcomes even as conflicting parties pursue strategies to address them (Eck, 2009). Within this psychological approach, leaders are likely to emphasise the use of national symbols, such as the flag, to evoke strong emotional reactions that, more often than not, translate into the automatic endorsement and support for policies likely to exacerbate parties' conflicts.

Negotiation and bargaining processes in international relations influence the outcomes of any existing conflicts. In most cases, the norms that govern political behaviour in conflicts extending over time have strongly encouraged the conflicting parties to adopt zero-sum thinking. As such, negotiation processes have taken ages as both parties are unwilling to make adjustments that could see the faster management of conflicts and their subsequent resolution for the good of all parties in the international arena. In these cases, the actions of the negotiation parties undermine the process even if they have committed themselves to a complete resolution of the issues within the negotiating table. The projected outcomes influence such actions in the negotiation process as leaders are afraid of being termed failures for accepting a particular position that seemingly puts their nation down. Additionally, negotiating parties are likely to form mirror images of the realities facing them as each party considers that the enemy harbours hostile intentions in the face of their vulnerabilities. At such times, the interactions between the conflicting parties result in self-fulfilling dynamics making it difficult for the parties to discover common and complementary interests (Odell, 2013).

Barriers to conflict resolution nand management are strengthened as the interaction between the parties further exacerbates, resulting in self-perpetuating dynamics characterising the continuous interactions between the conflicting parties. There is a need to overcome these barriers to attain peaceful coexistence among nations/states (Bar-Tal and Halperin, 2011). Here, states should promote various interaction strategies capable of reversing the conflict dynamics. Such strategies include applying problem-solving workshops to encourage parties to understand and penetrate their perspectives on the issues fuelling conflicts. At the macro level, the reversal of the conflict dynamics lies in the need to establish a new discourse among conflicting parties. This is characterised by the shift in emphasis from power politics characterised by threats and coercion to the adoption and implementation of mutual responsiveness, reciprocity in the negotiation process, and openness to support the establishment of new relationships.

Various psychological thoughts provide insights into psychology's different facets that promote identifying problems addressed in international relations theories. These include the need for states to identify and respond to threats to security, their ability to recognise opportunities while seeking to achieve more effective coordination, and the establishment of communities not easily influenced and driven by selfish nations' interests. Cognitive bias and error affect how decision-makers are held accountable with others remaining sceptical regarding their perceived enemies in the international arena (Caputo, 2013).

The prospect theory of international relations touches on the formulation of risk-taking capabilities among states, thus covering the importance of states maintaining the status quo while specifying the critical aspects of risk tolerance based on the perceived gains and losses in the interaction process. The theory of procedural and distributive justice also influences the psychological aspects of conflict and its resolution in the international arena. Here, scholars point out the morality of people, especially leaders, in making decisions and establishing policies that seek to meet the national interest while at the same time balancing with the global interest to ensure that no state/nation is adversely affected by such policies (Levy, 1997). The theory of cross-cultural psychology goes beyond people's thought processes, capturing the testable propositions on human relationships.

As initially developed by Amos Tversky and Daniel Kahneman (1992), respect theory offers an alternative to the expected utility theory in understanding human decision-making under risks and uncertainty. The prospect theory explains how individuals evaluate the available options before making suitable decisions based on their circumstances. It offers a reasonable explanation as to why people are likely to deviate from those decisions that could be considered rational from an observer's point of view. In international relations, the framing effect applies as individuals are likely to accept risks when faced with situations that are likely to result in losses and risk aversion when faced with circumstances associated with possible gains. The elements of the prospect theory are hard-wired into the human brain, informing choices based on the prevailing circumstances. This theory has often accounted for the anomalies linked to foreign policies across various states. In international relations, it is highly likely for states in the domain of losses to make irredentist decisions. At the same time, those within the dominion of gains are likely to accept the status quo.

The prospect theory also seeks to shed more light on the balance between deterrence and compliance regarding state actions in international relations. The theory points out that it would be more challenging to induce states into giving up on the things they already possess than preventing such states from taking those things they do not possess.

The structural realists acknowledge that as the number of great powers increases, there is an increasing likelihood of increased errors linked to the statecraft. As the number of great powers increases, the rate of uncertainty increases regarding which states will partner with others and how such relationships would benefit the parties involved. Here, the focus is not on static power distribution. Instead, the focus falls on the dynamic flow in the distribution of the ruling powers' economic, military, and technological capabilities at any given time.

According to the social-psychological aspects of international relations, conflicts are mainly driven by people's collective needs and fears and not merely by rational calculations and conceptions about interests. People focus on basic needs such as security and identity as perceived as the continued need for states' survival. As people fear that such basic needs may not be met due to the prevailing circumstances, they are likely to face existential fear, which is a crucial inhibitory factor in conflict resolution (Thies, 2001). For warring parties, reducing the intensity of their fighting or making concessions could endanger their survival hence the observed persistence of fights and conflicts in the international arena. Conflict resolution strategies adopted should meet the basic needs of the warring parties while reassuring that their fears are being met, thus penetrating to the level of individual needs.

Additionally, the social-psychological element of international relations posits that conflicts are an intersocial phenomenon rather than an interstate or intergovernmental one. International conflicts impact all levels of societies, including the economic, political, psychological, structural, and cultural aspects (Druckman, 2001). Political actors must seek to address the demands of their international opponents while addressing the effect of such conduct on its aspects of survival within communities. When states hold extremist views regarding resolving conflicts, there is a high chance that opportunities for amicable resolution are blocked. On the other hand, moderate factions are vital for creating opportunities for the warring parties to address their needs and arrive at a reasonable and acceptable conclusion for both parties. Additionally, the coalition of factions of a conflict is crucial for faster resolution of conflicts.

Another crucial element in international conflict revolves around the need for states to exercise influence at various levels. Here, players must avoid contests of coercive powers with an increasing focus on responsiveness to the other party's needs and fears. Using power and coercion in such circumstances creates retaliation and escalates conflicts (Burton, 1990). The most effective incentives in addressing conflicts at international levels include the premise for economic benefits, fair resource sharing, international approval and integration of institutions, and a general reduction in tension between conflicting parties and their supports in an international arena.

International conflicts cannot be just classified as a series of actions and reactions among the conflicting parties. Instead, it features interactive escalators and self-perpetuating dynamics that affect the parties to the conflicts and the situations that such parties go through. Conflicts result in various cognitive and perceptual biases, thus increasing and escalating the initial conflicts and creating a vicious cycle of escalation (Ross and Stillinger, 1991). This calls for the full involvement of parties to ensure that issues are addressed before they escalate into full-blown conflicts attracting both supporters and opponents, thus influencing international relations between the conflicting parties and their supporters and opponents.

Normative and perceptual processes are cited for conflict escalation in international relations. Normative processes are those that encourage conflict behaviour among parties. The existing fears as regards national survival and identity are crucial in conflict escalation. In such circumstances, the move towards conflict resolution is considered dangerously risky. These fears can also result in extreme violence as nations cite self-defence to meet their objectives and attain their goals as regards national interests. As such conflicts persist, leaders are likely to draw on the people's need for security and self-transcendence, thus mobilising intense group loyalty and producing overzealous adherence to the conflict norms as people seek to demonstrate their loyalties to the state or group. The move towards conflict de-escalation or efforts at reconciliation is seen as a weakness and in some circumstances, treated as treason.

On the other hand, normative processes limit the options available for consideration by decision-makers who constantly worry about being considered weak by the other parties to the conflict. Decision-makers are likelier to make choices based on readily available information and resources. As conflicts escalate, the resources supporting endless conflicting views seem readily available. At such times, decision-makers are likely to succumb to the group thinking that members should stick to the actions that are likely to maintain the group cohesiveness even though such actions could lead to conflict escalation. During negotiations towards conflict resolution, such members are more reluctant to raise questions, propose different approaches or even offer criticism to the popular opinions even if such does not help resolve conflicts.

Normative factors affect the negotiation process in conflict management. The persisting conflict norms pressure the negotiators into the zero-sum view in dispute management, holding that a gain for the opposing group amounts to losses for them. The fear of appearing weak in the negotiation makes them unwilling to make compromises even if such actions and decisions could promise a faster resolution and management of conflicts. According to Kelman (1997), conflicts create psychological and structural commitments among the conflicting parties, thus influencing actions and decisions on the part of the actors. Parties with their identity or economic interest vested in the conflicts may, for example, fight to maintain the status quo to protect such interests, thus leading to the protractions of such conflicts over extended periods. Other parties may commit to forestalling and compromise or settlement as the likelihood increases for people to incorporate conflicts into their worldview.

Perceptual processes in conflict management are crucial in the interpretation of conflict-related information. Conflicts make it difficult for parties to consider the perspectives and views of their opponents and as such, seem to be self-centred. Such parties are likely to develop mirror images of themselves and others with each party viewing themselves as excellent and peaceful compared to their opponents. They tend to justify their fighting as self-defence as the other side is considered aggressive and evil. Such misunderstandings further escalate conflicts as disconfirmation persists. Through selective exposure and recall, parties will likely avoid noticing any disconfirming information that could aid in speedy conflict resolution.

Consequences of Conflicts in International Relations

War and conflicts between nations extend beyond deaths and property loss witnessed in the immediate term. Armed conflicts have led to forced migrations as people seek security and safety away from their homelands. Other impacts include long-term refugee problems as well as the destruction of infrastructure. Additionally, nations' social, economic, and political institutions are often permanently damaged. The consequences of civil war are often felt in the developmental aspects of states and nations (Geis et al, 2015). Economic stability is closely linked to peace and stability within national boundaries. Several studies show a cause-effect relationship between armed conflict and war-torn countries' economic development and stability. Long-term effects of war include civilian suffering, thus impacting the overall productivity of an economy. The additional burden of death and disability is felt far beyond the end of active wars and conflicts between nations. Additionally, conflicts increase the population's exposure to diseases, also affecting the access to the supply of medical care and consequently impacting the health infrastructure, thus influencing the overall economy of nations.

Conflicts impose immeasurable levels of human suffering as regards economic and social costs. Immediate consequences include loss of human life, destruction of infrastructure, institutions, and human capital, political instability, and more significant uncertainties associated with the impact of conflicts on a nation's investment and economic growth (Adhikari, 2012). Conflicts also complicate public finances through the overall reduction of revenue collection due to the destruction of the tax base and the increase in military spending as nations seek to defend themselves and attain their national interest objectives. Fiscal deficits from conflicts, especially those that exacerbate wars, and the increasing likelihood of the rise in public debt, result in the shifting of resources from social and developmental spending, which results in the further deterioration of the standards of living and livelihoods of the affected population groups.

Potential spillover effects of conflicts are present primarily at regional levels. Conflicts could likely spill over to neighbouring states affecting the relationship of the warring nations with their neighbours. Indirect spillovers are associated with the depression of the economic activities in neighbouring states due to factors such as trade disruption and an increase in uncertainties, as well as the creation of social strains that adversely impact relationships. Even in the long run, the adverse effects of wars and conflicts are felt in the affected nations. Conflicts and fragility have negative consequences extending across generations and even for decades. Long after the fall of guns, consequences such as damaged human capital due to lowered productivity, weakened growth, and slow poverty reduction have been reported, especially among developing nations.

Conclusion

Delving into nationalism and its impact on international relations has been crucial in examining and justifying the behavior of nations in the design and implementation of their foreign policies. Naturally, nations seem to be selfish, seeking to pursue their interests without due concern for those of others. This concept has resulted in conflicts, affecting the relationship between nations in the international arena. An understanding of the concepts of nationalism is, therefore, crucial to enable readers to understand the factors that drive leaders in pursuing some of the leadership strategies to ensure that their citizens and followers obtain their desires through accomplished objectives and goals when it comes to national interests. However, it is vital to note that an individual's belonging to a nation is only circumstantial. This should, therefore, be used as something other than the main differentiating point to esteem one's own over others. Instead, nationalism should be applied as a uniting factor, bringing diversity and enabling people to embrace it for the optimal benefit of all parties involved

---

References

Adhikari, P (2012) 'The plight of the forgotten ones: Civil war and forced migration', *International Studies Quarterly*, 56(3), pp 590–606.

Ahmed, J. (2020). The theoretical significance of foreign policy in international relations-An analyses. *Journal of Critical Reviews*, 7(2), 707-792.

Ariely, G (2012) 'Globalization, immigration and national identity: How the level of globalization affects the relations between nationalism, constructive patriotism and attitudes toward immigrants?', *Group Processes & Intergroup Relations*, 15(4), pp 539–557.

Bar-Tal, D E and Halperin, E (2011) 'Socio-psychological barriers to conflict resolution.

Berezin, M. (2021). Identity, Narratives, and Nationalism', *Routledge Handbook of Illiberalism*. Routledge, pp 237–249.

Biersteker, T J (2013) 'State, sovereignty and territory', *Handbook of International Relations*, pp 245–272.

Brown, C (2009) 'Structural realism, classical realism and human nature', *International Relations*, 23(2), pp 257–270.

Brown, D (1998) Why Is the Nation-State so Vulnerable to Ethnic Nationalism?', *Nations and Nationalism*, 4(1), pp 1–15.

Burchill, S (2005) *The National Interest in International Relations Theory*. Springer.

Burns, A L (1961) 'Prospects for a general theory of international relations', *World Politics*, 14(1), pp 25–46.

Burton, J W (1990) 'Conflict Resolution', *Prevention*. New York: St. Martin's Press.

Caputo, A. (2013). A literature review of cognitive biases in negotiation processes. *International Journal of Conflict Management*.

Charnysh, V, Lucas, C, and Singh, P (2015) 'The ties that bind: National identity salience and pro-social behavior toward the ethnic other', *Comparative Political Studies*, 48(3), pp 267–300.

Connor, W (1993) 'Beyond reason: The nature of the ethnonational bond', *Ethnic and Racial Studies*, 16(3), pp 373–389.

Crawford, J and Crawford, J R (2006) *The Creation of States in International Law*. Oxford University Press.

Crawford, R M (2005) *Idealism and Realism in International Relations*. Routledge.

Crisher, B B (2021)' Territorial wars and absolute outcomes', *Research and Politics*, 8(3), 20531680211043316.

D'Anieri, P (1997) 'Nationalism and international politics: Identity and sovereignty in the Russian-Ukrainian conflict', *Nationalism and Ethnic Politics*, 3(2), pp 1–28.

De Cleen, B (2017) 'Populism and nationalism', *The Oxford Handbook of Populism*, 1, pp 342–262.

de Figueiredo Jr, R J and Elkins, Z (2003) 'Are patriots bigots? An inquiry into the vices of in-group pride', *American Journal of Political Science*, 47(1), pp 171–188.

Dimitrakis, P (2012) 'The Soviet invasion of Afghanistan: International reactions, military intelligence and British diplomacy', *Middle Eastern Studies*, 48(4), pp 511–536.

Donnelly, J (2000) *Realism and International Relations*. Cambridge University Press.

Druckman, D (2001) 'Nationalism and war: A social-psychological perspective', *Peace, Conflict, and Violence: Peace Psychology for the 21st Century*, pp 49–65.

Dumas, L J (1990) 'Economic power, military power, and national security', *Journal of Economic Issues*, 24(2), pp 653–661.

Eck, K (2009) 'From armed conflict to war: Ethnic mobilization and conflict intensification', *International Studies Quarterly*, 53(2), pp 369–388.

Fendrick, R J (2012) 'Diplomacy as an instrument of national power', *US Army War College Guide to National Security, Policy and Strategy*, pp 179–184.

Finnemore, M (1996) *National Interests in International Society*. Cornell University Press.

Geis, A, Fehl, C, Daase, C, and Kolliarakis, G (2015) 'Gradual processes, ambiguous consequences: rethinking recognition in international relations', *Recognition in International Relations*. Palgrave Macmillan, London, pp 3–26.

Gibler, D M (2012) *The Territorial Peace: Borders, State Development, and International Conflict*. Cambridge University Press.

Gleditsch, K S (2009) *All International Politics Is Local: The Diffusion of Conflict, Integration, and Democratization*. University of Michigan Press.

Guzzini, S (2013) *Realism in International Relations and International Political Economy: The Continuing Story of a Death Foretold*. Routledge.

Heiskanen, J (2019) 'Spectra of sovereignty: Nationalism and international relations', *International Political Sociology*, 13(3), pp 315–332.

Heiskanen, J (2021) 'Nations and Nationalism in International Relations', *Routledge Handbook of Historical International Relations*. Routledge, pp 244–252.

Heller, M (2011) *Paths to Post-Nationalism: A Critical Ethnography of Language and Identity*. Oxford University Press.

Hussak, L J and Cimpian, A (2019) '"It feels like it's in your body": How children in the United States think about nationality', *Journal of Experimental Psychology: General*, 148(7), 1153.

Jang, W Y, Hong, J, and Frederick, E (2015) 'The framing of the North Korean Six-Party Talks by Chinese and North Korean news agencies: Communist propaganda and national interests', *Media International Australia*, 154(1), pp 42–52.

Janz, D R (2020) 'Siebert on Nationalism as Pathology', *The Critique of Religion and Religion's Critique*. Brill, pp 202–210.

Jentzsch, C, Kalyvas, S N, and Schubiger, L I (2015) 'Militias in civil wars', *Journal of Conflict Resolution*, 59(5), pp 755–769.

Kadir, A, Shenoda, S, Goldhagen, J, Pitterman, S, Suchdev, P S, Chan, K J, . . . and Arnold, L D (2018) 'The effects of armed conflict on children', *Pediatrics*, 142(6).

Kaufmann, C (1996) 'Possible and impossible solutions to ethnic civil wars', *International Security*, 20(4), pp 136–175.

Keitner, C I (2012) *The Paradoxes of Nationalism: The French Revolution and Its Meaning for Contemporary Nation Building*. SUNY Press.

Kelman, H C (1997) 'Social-psychological dimensions of international conflict', *Peacemaking in International Conflict: Methods and Techniques*, pp 191–237.

Kiper, J, Gwon, Y, and Wilson, R A (2020) 'How Propaganda Works: Nationalism, Revenge and Empathy in Serbia', *Journal of Cognition and Culture*, 20(5), pp 403–431.

Kratochwil, F (1982) 'On the notion of "interest" in international relations', *International Organization*, 36(1), pp 1–30.

Lacher, H (2016) 'Making sense of the international system: The promises and pitfalls of contemporary Marxist theories of international relations', *Historical Materialism and Globalization*, Routledge, pp 147–164.

Lake, D A (2003) 'International relations theory and internal conflict: insights from the interstices', *International Studies Review*, 5(4), pp 81–89.

Lake, D A (2007) 'The state and international relations', Available at SSRN 1004423.

Lazeri, M (2020, December 1) *The Nation-State Is a Dogma: Methodological Nationalism and Assumption-Free Social Science*. International Migration, Integration and Social Cohesion-IMISCOE. https://www.imiscoe.org/news-and-blog/.

Lebow, R N (2007) *Coercion, Cooperation, and Ethics in International Relations*. Taylor & Francis.

Lerner, A B (2020) 'The uses and abuses of victimhood nationalism in international politics', *European Journal of International Relations*, 26(1), pp 62–87.

Lerner, A B (2022) 'Pathological nationalism? The legacy of crowd psychology in international theory', *International Affairs*, 98(3), pp 995–1012.

Levy, B S and Sidel, V W (2016) 'Documenting the effects of armed conflict on population health', *Annual Review of Public Health*, 37, pp 205–218.

Levy, J S (1997) 'Prospect theory, rational choice, and international relations'. *International Studies Quarterly*, 41(1), pp 87–112.

Liu, J H and Hilton, D J (2005) 'How the past weighs on the present: Social representations of history and their role in identity politics', *British Journal of Social Psychology*, 44(4), pp 537–556.

Machiavelli, N (2004) 'The prince', *YOUTH*, 1(3), pp 1–12.

McCrone, D and Bechhofer, F (2015) *Understanding National Identity.* Cambridge University Press.

McKay, S (1998) 'The effects of armed conflict on girls and women', *Peace and Conflict*, 4(4), pp 381–392.

Mearsheimer, J J (2007) 'Structural realism', *International Relations Theories: Discipline and Diversity*, 83, pp 77–94.

Mearsheimer, J J (2011, May) 'Kissing cousins: Nationalism and realism', *Yale Workshop on International Relations*, vol 5, pp 1–44.

Milioni, A (2022, July 9) *What Is Methodological Nationalism? — THE Pamphlet.* THE PAMPHLET. https://www.the-pamphlet.com/articles/methodological-nationalism.

Mingst, K A, McKibben, H E, and Arreguin-Toft, I. M (2018) *Essentials of International Relations.* WW Norton & Company.

Moir, L (2002) *The Law of Internal Armed Conflict*, vol 19. Cambridge University Press.

Morrow, J D (1999) 'The strategic setting of choices: Signaling, commitment, and negotiation in international politics', *Strategic Choice and International Relations*, 86, pp 86–91.

NYU Web Communications (nd). *Young Children May See Nationality as Biological, New Study Suggests.* NYU. https://www.nyu.edu/about/news-publications/news/2019/february/young-children-may-see-nationality-as-biological--new-study-sugg.html.

Odell, J (2013) 'Negotiation and bargaining', *Handbook of International Relations*, pp 379–400.

Olzak, S (2004) 'Ethnic and nationalist social movements', *The Blackwell Companion to Social Movements*, pp 666–693.

Paret, P (1993) *Understanding War: Essays on Clausewitz and the History of Military Power.* Princeton University Press.

Pottier, J (2002) *Re-imagining Rwanda: Conflict, Survival and Disinformation in the Late Twentieth Century*, vol. 102. Cambridge University Press.

Powell, R (2002) 'Bargaining theory and international conflict', *Annual Review of Political Science*, 5(1), pp 1–30.

Rice, C (2000) 'Promoting the national interest', *Foreign Aff*, 79, 45.

Robinson, T W and Shambaugh, D L (eds) (1995). *Chinese Foreign Policy: Theory and Practice.* Oxford University Press.

Ross, L and Stillinger, C (1991) 'Barriers to conflict resolution', *Negot J*, 7, 389.

Rovelli, C (2018, July 24) 'National identity is fake. We should focus on the wider common good', *The Guardian*. https://www.theguardian.com/commentisfree/2018/jul/24/national-identity-fake-toxic-intolerance-italy-fascism.

Rubinstein, A Z (1999) 'Alliances and Strategy: Rethinking Security', *World Affairs: The Journal of International Issues*, pp 58–76.

Sapolsky, R (2019) 'This is your brain on nationalism: The biology of us and them', *Foreign Aff*, 98, 42.

Schrock-Jacobson, G (2012) 'The violent consequences of the nation: Nationalism and the initiation of interstate war', *Journal of Conflict Resolution*, 56(5), pp 825–852.

Schulze, K E (2013) *The Arab-Israeli Conflict.* Routledge.

Smith, A D (1979) *Nationalism in the Twentieth Century.* Australian National University Press.

Smith, H (1990) The womb of war: Clausewitz and international politics', *Review of International Studies*, 16(1), pp 39–58.

Søndergaard, H (2003) 'Globalization and National Identity', *Media in a Globalized Society*, 91.

Stein, J G (2013) 'Psychological explanations of international decision making and collective behavior', *Handbook of International Relations*, pp 195–219.

Suddaby, R, Foster, W M, and Trank, C Q (2010) 'Rhetorical history as a source of competitive advantage', *The Globalization of Strategy Research*. Emerald Group Publishing Limited.

Taylor, D M and Moghaddam, F M (1994) *Theories of Intergroup Relations: International, Social, Psychological Perspectives*. Greenwood Publishing Group.

Thies, C G (2001) 'A social psychological approach to enduring rivalries', *Political Psychology*, 22(4), pp 693–725.

Tversky, A and Kahneman, D (1992) 'Advances in prospect theory: Cumulative representation of uncertainty', *Journal of Risk and Uncertainty*, 5(4), pp 297–323.

Van Evera, S (1994) 'Hypotheses on nationalism and war', *International Security*, 18(4), pp 5–39.

von Clausewitz, C (1976) 'Introduction to On War,' translated by Michael Howard and Peter Paret.

Williams, M C (2004) 'Why ideas matter in international relations: Hans Morgenthau, classical realism, and the moral construction of power politics', *International Organization*, 58(4), pp 633–665.

Zhuojun, W and Hualing, H (2014) 'National identity in the era of globalization: Crisis and reconstruction', *Social Sciences in China*, 35(2), pp 139–154.

CHAPTER 4

Introduction

Researchers in the psychology field have invested efforts and resources in finding the relationship between people's identities and their self-esteem. They note that an individual's esteem is linked to their sense of belonging to a nation and their position. The concept of self-esteem is derived from the position one's nation holds in the global arena and consequently informs people's behaviours and treatment towards their group and outsiders. Research exhibits that people from highly recognised and popular nations possess higher levels of esteem and stability vital in making informed decisions for the nation's good. Additionally, those originating from lowly considered nations are more likely to have a lower sense of esteem and could be aggressive as they seek to defend their national boundaries against attacks. This results in conflicts between people across national boundaries, yet they are more factors that could keep human beings together instead of separating them. Self-esteem and national identity also influence people's conduct and inform factors such as xenophobia, the dislike and likely attacks of the outgroups, ingroup evaluation, and favouritism. Additionally, the concept explains the levels of conflict in societies and the underlying factors while supporting policymakers in adopting policies suitable for addressing conflicts and promoting the peaceful coexistence of people despite any differentiating characteristics.

Nationalism at Individual and National Levels

Nationalism is defined at individual and national levels. At the individual level, it refers to the attitude that a person exhibits towards another one sharing national identity on the one hand and another one who is considered a stranger to the prevailing beliefs, norms, and way of life. This is a psychological point of view as clear guidelines cannot define the conduct. On the national level, nationalism is defined based on the actions taken by nations to assert self-determination from other nations (Dekker, Malová, and Hoogendoorn, 2003). National identity, a concept esteemed in nationalism, refers to common origin, culture, or ethnicity among individuals. The fact is often associated with the level of allegiance one has for their homeland.

At the individual level, the concept of the home informs a person's attitudes and perceived association with others. The home is considered a psychologically critical concept. It refers to both the physical home and the feelings associated with belonging to one's homeland. At home, an individual is assured of security, familiarity, and privacy. Psychologists consider attachment to one's home a crucial sentiment (Etherington, 2010). Such places emphasis on the attachment to one's home and family from an earlier age. In environmental psychology, place-bound affection explains individuals' positive feelings toward their homes and places of origin. As such, people are likely to maintain closeness to their homeland.

At national levels, on the other hand, a nation is referred to as a cultural group that other factors could unite in addition to descent as well as the one endowed by the presence of civic ties. The concept of a nation covers the physical location and place and represents the ethnic compositions and perceptions of individuals living within the identified national boundaries. The feelings associated with nationalism at the national level include those of protection, familiarity, and security (Reeskens and Wright, 2013). In this case, individuals often associate the home with the nation in the psychological assessment of the terms. Notions of nationalism are, therefore, in part reason and other feelings. Therefore, they consist of the physical reality of the concepts and the projection of feelings associated with such terms and concepts.

Nationalism is considered a powerful political force that has allowed states and their established institutions to shape the lives of citizens from afar. The nation-state has become the major player in political organizations across established democracies. Accordingly, various researchers define nationalism using various components that seek to explain and point out the behaviour of individuals and groups within and outside identified national boundaries. State-building nationalism, according to researchers, seeks to impose a cultural homogeneity among people within identified national borders (Wimmer and Glick Schiller, 2002). Here, benefits accrue for individuals who agree to join in the majority cultures within the identified regions and nations. Such benefits revolve around political and economic growth associated with the support for the majority culture as expressed in the use of language and adherence to the majority group's norms, values, and cultures. Such a move is not a problem for the majority group members since it occurs for their advantage.

It, however, affects minority groups as individuals here are forced to adapt to foreign cultures and ways of life that may not go well with their belief systems and norms. As such, the minority groups could choose to assimilate and become members of the dominant nation. Nevertheless, in most circumstances, resistance exists as each group seeks to fight for its interest and pursue those elements and ideologies that seem to sit well with them (Brading,1994). When minority nationals seem to resent and resist the need to neglect their cultures and languages, conflicts arise between the majority and the minority groups, thus resulting in competition and the need to push one's group interests above those of others. Here, a peripheral form of nationalism arises where distinct cultural groups seek to establish nations of their own as characterised by the pursuance of the elements of autonomy.

While some groups act assimilation as a means through which they may achieve peaceful coexistence in the face of diverse group interests, others are adamant about maintaining their ways of life despite the existing power struggles (Ma,1992). Members of smaller groups are more likely to find assimilation into the majority cultures more reasonable than the assimilation rate among larger groups that are likely to resist such urges yet still survive in the highly competitive and dynamic world. Unification nationalism is cited in cases where members of one nation are scattered across different states.

National Identity and Self

Defence of one's nation is one of the few commitments for which individuals would kill others or even surrender their own lives. The psychological roots of the power of nationalism are yet to be studied in detail. The segregation of individuals into national groups based on the need to attain survival and protective functions was thus considered essential for national identity (Spinner-Halev and Theiss-Morse, 2003). A sense of national identity is closely linked to the need for research into the historical experiences of wounds and hurts inflicted by one group upon others in a pluralistic society. Any myths that touch on national origins are crucial for understanding how to maintain cohesion among individuals and communities and their cohesion.

The relationship between national identity and self-identity determines the extent to which patriotic feelings attain. National identity allows individuals to define and locate themselves relative to the world. Through this concept, individuals have been known to be willing to surrender their interests in favour of those of the nation as well as curtail the interests of others in pursuance of national interest. One significant explanation for why humans search for meaning is the need to escape the despair over their mortality (Gong, 2007). Dedicating one's life to fighting for one's nation is considered a modern secular similar to religion since the nation is immortal and will live beyond human lives. This explains individuals' extreme loyalty and identification towards their nation-states.

Conflicts among national groups are particularly intense, especially when sectarian differences are involved. Important contributors to the conduct of individuals in a group include the feeling of self (Reicher and Hopkins, 2000). Other critical aspects relating to the influence of self in group conduct conclude the effect of self on groups, nationalistic emotions, and self-feeling as well the aspects of survival, self-worth, and value.

Liberal nationalism is crucial in pushing people towards the understanding of nationality in people's lives while focusing on the implementation and justification of any liberal policies put in place. According to liberal nationalists, the concept of national identity is considered the basic human need compatible with the elements of individuality and equality, as well as promoting those ideals aimed at the flourishing and functionality of states. Liberalists tie the concept of nationalism to self-esteem. The liberal theory of nationalism sought to provide a framework in which people could satisfy their national aspirations without getting involved in violent acts and decisions (Tamir,1995). Liberals also link the concept of an individual's self-respect to their national communities. This is based on the argument that the individual is also affected when the nation's identity is demeaned.

When national identities are nested, likely, the minority nations may not strive for more autonomy. When nationalities are rivals, on the other hand, minority nations are more likely to seek more autonomy. It is evident from the nations' research that the oppressed nations or minorities are more likely than not to fight for the recognition and acknowledgement of their national interests (Medrano and Gutiérrez, 2001). Such minority groups find the rule by others to insult their autonomy, causing a sense of wounded pride and humiliation. Minority groups crave the status of independence from other nations and the need to be self-ruling. Meaningful recognition and status among national groups are crucial for their sovereignty.

Liberal theorists, on the other hand, argue that national communities must defend themselves as they serve the interests and needs of communities, thus ensuring that they attain self-respect. These theorists further argue that if an individual belongs to a nation that does not command much respect from other nationalities, then the individual's self-respect will be undermined in the process (Charney, 2003). National membership is a constitutive factor of the personal identities of the individuals counted in. As such, the self-image of individuals is affected by the status of their national community. Thus, the ability of individuals within national boundaries to lead a satisfactory life is founded on the ability of members to view themselves as active members of worthy communities. Consequently, a dignified, safe, and flourishing national existence is crucial for the well-being of individuals crucial factor for group membership is that members view their self-esteem and well-being as being closely affected by the success and failures of the group as a whole. Therefore, self-respect is crucial for people to lead a satisfying life.

National cultures are considered crucial because people's self-respect is closely linked to the level of esteem in which their national group is held. This means that individuals are likely to display low esteem levels if a specified culture is not respected. National identity is essential for giving people meanings in their lives. It is vital in enabling individuals to secure their sense of self-respect, belonging, and security fundamental to their values as humans. While this connection might not hold for everyone, it does for most people as it is suspected to lie deep in the human condition tied up with how humans seek to make sense of the world. Researchers further seek to link self-respect and esteem, citing that an individual with self-respect possesses a sense regarding the plans in one's life that are worth pursuing.

Consequently, self-respect is a special consideration worth pursuing among individuals. Individual dignity and self-respect require that groups and their memberships contribute significantly to an individual's sense of identity. As such, the unique identities of individuals should be generally respected and not made subjects of ridicule, discrimination, persecution, or hate despite the classification of an individual in terms of descent, belongingness, and associations with others.

Researchers discuss the elements of self-determination and respect among encompassing groups. This further emphasizes that individuals can have self-respect in cases where their nations are respected. Thus, a secure identification with a group becomes a paramount element worth pursuing as individuals and nations seek to pursue their interests in the face of diverse individual and communal needs (Buttle, 2000). According to researchers in the field, self-respect is considered a fundamental liberal value as it points out the dignity that citizens deserve in liberal states and the fact that such dignity is a precondition for individual and group well-being and welfare (Margalit and Raz, 1990). Consequently, studies show that a nation gives individuals dignity, thus engaging their self-worth. In the contemporary world, nations give individual dignity through which their self-respect is engaged. This argument gives nationalism its emotive powers placing it in the register of pride and humiliation. Thus, a group's dignity lies in identified categorical identity. Then when this is threatened, individuals within this category are also threatened, leading to feelings of positive self-worth and resulting in retaliation and responses that could steer conflicts and disagreements among groups as each seeks to defend their dignity and self-respect.

Nationalism is considered a crucial part of the sought-for dignity among individuals. This points out the fact that no identity is completely inwardly formed. As such, a nation or group significantly influences an individual's esteem and self-respect as expressed in the form of dignity shared with a collective group of individuals. Therefore, the search for dignity is an outward quest, resulting in the conclusion that individuals gain dignity when their nations are recognized as equal or even more superior to others.

Identity and Extremism

The contemporary world is pervaded by extremism as defined by one-dimensional ideologies and world views, conspiracy theories, and ethnocentric prototypes that influence how individuals and groups interact with others. Other elements of extremism include stigma and social exclusion, destructive popular unrest, terrorism, and collective violence. Individual belief systems and behaviours are associated with uncertainty about the world in general and one's place in it (Stephens, Sieckelinck & Boutellier, 2021). Research shows that occurrences such as genocides can be closely linked to conditions of acute uncertainties in society.

Social psychologists have invested their efforts in determining whether there is a link between group identification and hostility or prejudice. In the past, researchers did not find any meaningful connection. They, therefore, sought to assess the conditions under which higher levels of identification with one's group were linked to greater discrimination and apathy expressed towards other groups.

Extremist rhetoric provides the link between hostility and identification. The extremists seek to foster group consciousness based on the essentialised cultural and spiritual scientific discourses that bring people together. Here, there is an element where the subordination of individual interests for group benefits is evident (Hogg, 2014). Thus, individuals express their commitment to the group through unlimited support toward achieving group objectives. Groups take precedence over other aspects of individual lives as expressed in a commitment to duty and honour. For extremists, the party is considered a true embodiment of the interests and spirit of the people.

Individual consciousness about the group is associated with victimhood, where a threat to the existence and continuity of nations is felt—threats to nations and group existence influence and impact the people's survival. Racism is closely associated with the threat where members of minority groups are portrayed as having committed crimes taking housing and jobs supposedly belonging to the nationals, and eroding the cultural traditions of aboriginal groups. As a result of the perceived threats between groups and nations, there is an increasing likelihood for people to commit acts of hostility toward others and the perception and maintenance of physical and social boundaries between groups (Fearon and Laitin, 2000). Additionally, there is an increased likelihood of maintaining oppressive relations with such being legitimised by the threats.

Identity has been cited as one of the critical factors that predict, stimulate, and separate the engagement of individuals in activist groups. Once individuals become active members in identified groups, their identities are strengthened, and their identities become fused with group identity. Consequently, extremists are likely to cut themselves off from external contacts and become increasingly committed to the group norms and aims.

In diverse contexts, belongingness, meaning, and control are fundamental to human life. Any challenges and limitations to the individual sense of identity and self create significant distress in the individual. An essential component of the individual's sense of belonging is closely linked to the social groups one identifies with, beliefs, attitudes, and affiliations. According to the social identity theory, individuals are often committed to maintaining positive intergroup distinctiveness. They are likely to go to extreme lengths to maintain the belief that their groups are superior to others (De Vries and Van Kersbergen, 2007). They are likely to go to extreme ends even to engage in antisocial behaviours that could risk individual safety while seeking to maintain the group's prestige.

Feelings of perceived injustices in the social setting, humiliation, threats, and fears are viewed through group lenses and likely provoke a collective response. When the sense of threat is at the group level, the community focuses on defending itself and is willing to hurt others. Here, the group members are perceived as sharing a common fate and being endowed with fixed and unchanging attributes vital for defending their interests in the face of conflicts, injustices, and discrimination (Charkawi, Dunn, and Bliuc, 2021). When such feelings arise among group members, there is a likelihood that self-essentialisation in the group is felt as collective action is pursued to enhance the feelings of similarity and groupness in the threatened faction. The increase in the level of outgroup bias, xenophobia, and the engagement of groups and individuals in violent extremism complements such processes.

Researchers have pointed out the role of essentialist identities in pushing individuals toward violent extremism through the analysis of the uncertainty identity theory. They note that the feelings of uncertainty concerning the world and an individual's place in it could be unsettling. Individuals, therefore, counteract these feelings by adopting self-categorisation and social identity processes (Abrams and Hogg, 2010). These feelings drive the fundamentalist perspectives, ethnic revivals, and populist national groups that are crucial in providing a sense of self in the uncertain contemporary world. Self-categorisation results in depersonalisation; thus, the ingroup prototype is now considered crucial to the person's identity (Ferguson and McAuley, 2021).

Self-categorisation affects an individual's sense of identity with a group and their feelings and behaviours to conform to the ingroup prototype. The process attracts consensual validation of individual attitudes, behaviours, and feelings towards ingroup and outgroup members. Thus, group identification reduces the uncertainty about who individuals are and how they should act and respond to the group members and outsiders. The effectiveness of groups in reducing feelings of uncertainty is, however, based on group structures. Those groups that effectively reduce uncertainty are distinctive, unambiguous, clearly defined, and characterised by tightly shared prototypes (Hornsey, 2008). Thus, members interact and share group attributes and goals vital for making informed and acceptable decisions for all its constituents. Their role in reducing uncertainties creates a higher need for members to join such organised groups at all costs. In the extreme, members are likely to follow group interests even if such can lead to conflicts with other groups.

Uncertainty-identity theory points out the role of self-uncertainty in group processes and how various groups relate to each other. The theory acknowledges that people identify with groups to reduce feelings of uncertainty. Such feelings have been cited as creating a hydraulic motivational state that drives people to actions and decisions to reduce such uncertainties. As such, they seek to belong to groups through self-categorisation, especially when such groups are distinctive and clearly defined by consensual norms (Hogg, 2007). This also points out the elements of group extremism in conditions of uncertainty where people strive to belong to hierarchically and structured groups that are associated with strong and authoritative leadership that could focus on achieving their interests at the expense of others. Self-categorisation transforms an individual's self-conception as individuals seek to obtain their self-image by focusing on group prototype that describes how they think, feels, ad do, who they are and how they interact with others.

Group belongingness also influences the validation of individuals from ingroup members, thus dealing with the self-uncertainties affecting individuals. As individuals identify with well-structured groups, the world becomes more predictable (Hogg and Adelman, 2013). Groups are associated with a range of phenomena that can be used to explain human behaviour, such as social influences, norms, deviance from group culture, minority influences, extremism, leadership processes, and ideological orthodoxy that impacts how groups interact with each other.

National Pride

National pride refers to the positive effect the public feels towards their country due to their national identity. It is the sense of esteem that an individual derives from their identity and the sense of esteem towards their nation. Some researchers refer to national pride as emotions associated with the national collective. The term best describes an individual and the personal experience associated with the collective entity of the nation. The aspect is complicated by the availability of social construction of the national identity through the process of inventing and imagining one's position relative to the nation (Solt, 2011). This means that individuals are in the pursuit of constructing the nation's identity even as they derive meaning and pride from it. Individuals with high levels of national pride engage in cooperative actions for the good of the nation. Such deeds include purchasing goods manufactured within a nation's borders, prescribing and shunning some activities that relate to or go against the national norms, respectively, and being prepared to serve in the country's military. Studies in economics and social sciences show that national pride is crucial for encouraging cooperation for the benefit of the group while yielding substantial benefits from the group members by providing essential goods and services and solutions to the challenges facing individuals within national boundaries (Landau, 2020). On the other hand, an overabundance of national pride has been cited for the worst atrocities in history.

Nations remain independent even though the world has become one global village because the political process is not yet globalised. This means that government officials and politicians must still be considered citizens of the nations they represent. Successful multicultural teaming in the face of globalization is crucial as characterised by collaboration and cooperation of individuals despite their differentiating features. Even in the face of globalisation, people may fail to appreciate the need for collaboration and togetherness, instead pointing out the element of threat to the prevailing cultural identity leading to an increased sense of nationalism among people with similar descent and interests as compared to those who lack any common features. As globalization permeates every level of society and national boundaries, many countries gain comparative advantage with the national pride characterized by their capability to trade in the global marketplace (Machida, 2012). While a greater level of trust in one's national government generates a positive externality increasing the level of trust for international organisations, the losers from the globalisation process could become resentful, further fuelling feelings of national separateness.

Individuals perceive the social construction of national pride and can identify with it as part of their self-concept. These individuals express a sense of pride and shame associated with their national pride. An individual is aware of who shares the same identity as part of one's group and thus feels a sense of loyalty and duty to contribute towards the welfare and well-being of the group. The national ride can be analysed through two dimensions: patriotism and nationalism. Patriotism showcases the positive, cohesive, and cooperative side of the nation's pride while nationalism exhibits the exclusive, hostile, and derogating side of national pride. The differences between the two viewpoints are associated with the extent of superiority and pride one feels toward their home country (Britt and Heise, 2000). Patriotism results in a neutral and benign love for one's country, characterised by ingroup love and not necessarily outgroup hate and exclusion. Nationalism, on the other hand, features competitiveness between nations that could lead to outgroup hate and exclusion for people who do not share dissimilar characteristics to one's group. Patriotism features self-referential feelings while nationalism is expressed in terms of the comparative advantage of one nation over others with one nation exhibiting feelings of superiority above others. Another crucial differentiating feature between the positive and negative aspects of national pride lies in how outsiders are treated in nationalism is prejudicial and downwardly comparative. It can trigger negative feelings and consequences in the relationships between in-groups and out-groups.

According to psychologists, a nation is regarded as a surrogate parent while the experience of sharing national pride with others is considered colourful, emotional, and exciting, an analysis of nationalism in the face of national pride, however, shows that people who are dysfunctional and who are in pursuit of bonding with authority figures are more likely to act toward xenophobic protection of their nation's states (Nussbaum, 1994). Attachment to one's s nation might also act as a parental replacement, bringing to mind the references to one's fatherland or motherland. Psychological theorists regard attachments as a vital part of personality development, affecting individuals' ability to love and enjoy healthy relationships. As such, one's country and family are major components of identity. Thus, to threaten the family of nations is regarded by many as a threat to one's integrity of the self.

Some theories have been pursued to assess individuals' likelihood of being prejudiced toward competition with others. The authoritarian personality theory posits that some human personalities are more predisposed to prejudice than others. The authoritarian personality, as described by Adorno, refers to an individual who has extreme respect for authority and is more likely to be obedient to those who hold power over them (Duckitt, 2005). It was based on the need for researchers to understand more about factors that led people towards committing atrocities and the markers that indicated the presence of personality traits that could be measured and identified as possible links to abuse of power, violence, and others issues associated with lawlessness and war.

Current research into these aspects features personality traits tied to law-breaking behaviour, including a lack of empathy and rigidity. The focus on personality theories revolves around components associated with strong adherence to conventional values aligned to political ideologies based on the prevailing socioeconomic backgrounds. People with authoritarian personalities also exhibit deference towards authority figures and the insistence on obedience from the people ranked as belonging to the lower status and cadres in society. Additionally, such individuals exhibit hostility towards people with different belief systems or backgrounds (Adorno et al, 2019). Such hostility is often expressed through physical violence and elements of bullying and mocking.

Realistic conflict theory, on the other hand, features the perception of zero-sum competition resulting in the likelihood of individuals feeling threatened. The theory attempts to explain why negative stereotypes, prejudice, and discrimination are developed and expressed toward members of other social groups. Thus, the theory explains the possibility of conflict between groups of people with differing goals and those competing for limited resources (McKenzie and Gabriel, 2017).

Frustration-aggression theory, on the other hand, is the individual psychological version of the realistic conflict theory in which an individual fails to achieve the desired goals and thus develops feelings of aggression towards others. The theory is based on the psychodynamic explanation of catharsis (Breuer and Elson, 2017). Psychologists proposing this theory believed that the drive for individual aggression was innate, and there was a need to release the build-up of frustration. This is achieved through sublimation or displacement, where aggression is directed toward something or someone. This could be used to explain the element of aggression by individuals towards others who are classified as outsiders or foreigners.

Another crucial theory in explaining national pride relates to the social dominance theory, in which individuals with higher status are more likely to make decisions that uphold and preserve their status instead of meeting the needs of those with lower status. The theory could explain the tendency of nationalistic leaders to make decisions that support them in meeting their needs without regard for the interests of citizens or followers (Sidanius and Pratto, 2012). Consequently, the masses are involved in conflicts and required to act according to the leader's direction despite the fact that such direction may not benefit the masses.

Other crucial elements of prejudice and discrimination related to political conservatism. According to research, lower intelligence levels among individuals were linked to higher outgroup prejudice. It was highly likely that individuals with lower cognitive abilities were attracted to right-wing ideologies that promote order and coherence (Chambers, Schlenker, and Collisson, 2013). Since such ideologies emphasised the need for nations and groups to maintain the status quo, they were likely to promote outgroup prejudice. The willingness of individuals to go to war was exhibited in the concepts of national pride and ideologies associated with the norms of specified nations to support and defend one's country in order to attain the desired national interests (Walter, 2017). Research also showed that the elements of authoritarian personality and personal frustration were vital for prejudice and discrimination against the outgroups.

Research into the national pride levels of various countries showcases various perspectives on nations' conduct and foreign policies to determine their relationship and interactions with others. The research shows that national pride is the greatest among stable, established, and developed democracies. On the other hand, the level of national pride was lowest among ex-socialist states and countries afflicted by ethnic conflicts and war guilt (Fabrykant and Magun, 2019). Among the nations studied in the research, the United States of America remained a superpower regarding national pride based on its self-image and perception of itself among citizens and other key stakeholders in the international arena. This was based on the fact that the country's idealism positively supported individual and collective objectives. As one pursued national interest, their desires were also met (Fabrykant and Magun, 2016).

National pride is a factor of country-level factors and individual characteristics of countries. The level of national pride decreases with generations from the pre-world war cohorts to the current generation groups. It is believed that the decline in the level of pride is based on the dilution of nationalism as a result of globalisation and multilateralism, as well as the reaction to aggressive nationalism that resulted in wars and loss of lives in the past. National pride also seemed to decline among national minorities. In some of the cases, the minorities seemed to identify themselves with external nationalities based on their descent. In some instances, the level of pride among the minority groups was attributed to the discrimination and inequalities that had been meted out against them by the majority within the national boundaries (Tilley and Heath, 2007).

Research into the conduct of nations showcases the concept of humiliation as the major driving factor for the behaviour of nations in the international arena. Highly charged emotional states among leaders influence the outcomes of policies as reflected in the bias of policies to the detriment of more reasoned choices. Men's conduct in war requires leaders to restore self-worth and achieve triumph in all situations without losing face in the international arena. Such leaders are likely to favour aggressive foreign policies to avoid humiliation and shame due to failure to act on the issues affecting a country's citizens (Zapotoczny, nd). For states, humiliation associated with dependency and defeat characterizes the ultimate degradation of nations.

The psychological analysis of national choices in defending their interests points out the crucial element of humiliation in informing actions and decisions. People fight to avoid the humiliation of being crushed, overwhelmed by the force of being threatened with psychological annihilation. There is a high chance that fights and wars stem from the need for nations to maintain their pride in the face of conflicting interests (Allen, 2017). Militancy in the Middle East regions, for example, has been fuelled by the pervasive sense of humiliation among the involved states. Nations are likely to endorse or justify acts of violence against others if such are aimed at saving the nation's face. Such nations are likely to point out the irrational behaviours of their enemies and opponents while judging their extreme actions as just and necessary.

The rate at which America dominates other nations is attributed to the country's high degree of patriotic pride. The country takes pride in its supremacy of the democratic system and governance, showcasing itself as a country with fair-minded egalitarian people and assuming that the

American way of life bears a universal appeal to all people (Pei, 2003). Such fictions regarding one's country warrant a specified self-image and extol the virtues of superiority, moral authority, and uniqueness among nations. Consequently, preserving virtue and status is a crucial consideration and factor for nations. These attitudes, however, have been cited as crucial contributors to proclivity and violence among national groups as each seeks to defend their interests without regard for those of others.

The nation that overvalues pride as a sign of self-respect and worthiness dreads public humiliation and is likely to pursue all strategies to avoid such. In such instances, maintaining a positive self-image becomes one of the key objectives pursued to attain national interests (Jáuregui, 2000). When external groups challenge such opinions regarding the nation, such are considered jealous of the nation's achievement and are therefore shunned or oppressed, leading to aggression and violence in extreme forms. Dissenters of specific beliefs and norms at the national level are often regarded as outsiders and are likely to be cut off from the nation.

While some researchers attribute actions of violence to low self-esteem, others believe that an inflated belief of oneself or one's nation is more likely to trigger a violent group response. According to researchers, severe violence is likely to occur when a group perceives its superior position as being threatened or eroded by a rising rival group (Ostrowsky, 2010). It is evident from the research that aggressive, violent, and criminal groups share the beliefs of their superiority and could retaliate and respond if such are violated.

The more a social group overvalues pride as a sense of worthiness and self-respect, the more such a group dreads stigma and public humiliation. Nations seek to maintain a positive self-image among their citizens at all times, and they are likely to adopt strategies that enable them to retain such an image among their citizens as well as other stakeholders (Gray, 2005). When such a high opinion of the nation is challenged by opposing groups, leaders will seek to soothe the wounded egos by pointing out the jealousy of the dissenting group and requiring its followers to act by retaliating against the dissenting voices in extreme cases.

Researchers in psychology have linked the concepts of self-esteem and aggression. Counsellors, teachers, and social workers across the globe have been persuaded to think that improving young people's self-esteem could be a solution to curbing violent behaviours among them while promoting social and academic success (Velotti et al, 2017). Does the same apply to nations? However, research showed that high esteem could be an important cause of aggression compared to low self-esteem. Researchers studied the lives of prominent people known to have caused wars between nations, including Hitler and Saddam Hussein among others, concluding that the studied individuals did not show any signs of low self-esteem. Instead, they were attributed to the high esteem of self with the capacity to influence others into joining in their aggression and pursuits to achieve the desired outcomes (Baumeister, 2001). From the research, it was evident that self-esteem alone could not be attributed to the aggression and violence occurring in the world. Instead, threatened egoism was a factor that promoted adverse actions by leaders across nations, causing bloodshed and the loss of property.

It is evident from the research that people like to think well of themselves. If such an opinion of themselves is criticised or questioned, they are likely to respond through aggression to shut down the dissenting voices. The inflated, tenuous, and unstable forms of high self-esteem were likely to be highly affected by negative criticism. This was the same for nations. Leaders with a high sense of esteem sought to pursue national interests at all costs without due regard for the interests of others. When such stances were questioned, leaders were likely to influence the masses into fighting to defend their positions leading to sustained conflicts and wars between national groups.

Evolution of Nationalism

The evolution of nationalism over the decades has been associated with the prevailing circumstances. While the concept has been suppressed at times, at other times, it has been used by nations to their advantage in justifying their actions and reactions based on the prevailing circumstances. Following the pre-world war period, the political philosophy of nationalism seemed to have been buried and ignored as nations in the European region sought to live in harmony through the formation of an international body that took all their interests into account, the European Union (Dinan, 2014). Here, the slogan was the coming together of nations through the creation of a unifying factor in which nations worked towards getting richer together by considering and acting on the interests of individual nations without pushing or fighting for the interests of only a few individuals or nations. Here, the objective was to unify nations while seeking to lose the national sovereignty that had resulted in wars and revolutions among nations in the past (Solberg, 2021). After the second world war, nationalism seemed defeated as nations sought to emerge and survive the adverse effects of the bloodshed and loss of property and people's livelihoods witnessed in the war.

Students of nationalism have established that there could be groups that, through their shared characteristics, could have formed unique nations yet have failed to create a sense of nationhood. Some of the reasons for the situation include the failure of leaders to mobilise the masses, the unavailability of cultural institutions to bring the people together, and the integration of the segments of people in communities to form a larger population with different interests altogether. This points out the fact that nationalistic movements succeed in attracting members because they have been able to generate a consensus regarding the nature of the community, define the community's boundaries, and consequently identify the domain elements of the identified identity. Groups have therefore created imagined communities presented as homogeneous even if it is composed of alike people.

According to research, the success of nationalism has been attributed to the pervasiveness of the collective reference leading to the adoption of imagined community's symbols and characteristics based on a belief system. The existence of common interests, norms, and a belief system is crucial for sustained cohesion among communities and for creating a sense of political loyalty among the masses (Risse, 2002). This further explains why nationalism is considered a unifying force among individuals of different nations yet could be potentially divisive inside states.

Research on nationalism also touches on the crucial role of identity in informing nationalistic sentiments and behaviour. Some researchers note that identity could remain salient or politically mobilised based on the events occurring or triggers that could awaken such nationalistic feelings among individuals. It is well noted that without a dominant collective identity, it would be impossible for an identified group of humans to develop nationalistic feelings. This further explains why a group is driven and sustained by a shared representation of collectivity. As such, a group is represented in the minds of the people by the presence of well-defined and sustainable salient features. Such markers include language, religion, and race of people's traditions based on the foundational features of group identity. These domains of identity, according to sociologists, are crucial for filtering experiences, interpreting them, and enabling individuals to build and define any immediate reality to serve as the foundation for future actions and decisions. Existing literature shows that such domains of identity inform the prevailing social and political processes in communities and nations. They inform the behaviour of individuals at their levels as well as within collective boundaries while creating a sense of belongingness to identified groups. The existence of collective identity is supported by collective beliefs shared by members of an identified group.

Collective identities are articulated and expressed through the mobilisation of individuals in social organisations and movements. Collective action is evident as individuals develop a sense of belonging to an identified group and the positive collaboration and interaction with other members resulting in the continuity of the identified group features. Personal experiences also make individuals feel and acknowledge that they share a particular set of features with others that may not be common for those considered outgroups. Additionally, institutions play a crucial role as identity builders. Political institutions design and promote the adoption of policies that guide constituents, thus creating a sense of belongingness for its members and enabling the sustainability of communities at large. The building of identities is greatly influenced by the belief system of politicians and leaders regarding imagined communities (Coller, 2006).

A passionate investment in one's country is not just a neutral factor. It negatively influences individuals' way of life while influencing their interactions in a multi-ethnic and multi-national setting. Nationalistic people and communities aim to win at all costs. They seek power and superiority as their only goals with the justification of hurting other people based on their ability to attain these goals. Instead of pursuing morality, long-term stability, and mutual benefit, nationalistic individuals pursue selfishness and a will to power (Mansbridge, 1990). This becomes the driving force that influences foreign policies and interactions in the international arena. This results in broken agreements, violence in communities, indifference to the suffering of others, and other harmful practices that destabilise nations and global politics. The consequences of global security associated with elements of nationalism could be disastrous within nations and in the international arena.

Nationalism also affects the way of life within nations. Although nationalistic leaders seek to pursue national interests to attain self-determination, such pursuits could result in internal fragmentation and instability. Within nations, nationalism pushes leaders towards determining who truly belongs to the nation and those now classified as outsiders. This encourages exclusionary and prejudiced approaches in policy making and treating others even within a nation's borders.

Nationalistic leaders feel entitled to break the laws of their own countries to suit their needs. In cases where the constitution interferes with nationalist ambitions, they are likely to choose their ambitions over the rule of law. Such occurrences are evident in how leaders control the media, interfere with the judiciary, and consequently conduct unlawful torture on civilians without due observance of the governing bodies and institutions in the country (Bechhofer and McCrone, 2009). Other harmful practices associated with nationalism include extrajudicial murders within national borders for individuals considered outsiders to a given nation and the imprisonment of supporters of political rivals in a nationalistic country. While none of the above actions is lawful and legal, nationalists feel the power to make such decisions without observing the need for them to provide a safe and secure environment for all the people within the national boundaries.

According to nationalistic leaders, any thoughtful and responsive governance structures interfere with the elements of self-glorification. As such, the leaders feel that any internal reflection among citizens and external criticism from external bodies and individuals must be squashed. Nationalist leaders are more likely than not to attack and disempower their opponents to destroy social movements that oppose their ways of life. Silencing criticism and oozing voices within a nation are dangerous as it removes any checks and measures of monitoring the country's existing governance structures. When a country and its leaders consider itself superior to its competitors, they acknowledge the wilfulness to inflict pain and suffering on citizens of other countries or those considered outsiders. The capability for a country to commit itself to pre-eminence and do whatever it takes is considered immoral, unlawful, or destructive.

Some factors that led to the re-emergence of nationalism include the Balkan wars of the 1990s, the economic crisis, and the impact of globalisation. The German nationalism witnessed before the second world war resulted in most of the European countries placing safeguards in their constitutions to prevent extremist parties and individuals from accessing political powers following the abuse of such powers in the past. However, the Balkan wars revealed that such measures were inefficient in achieving the desired objectives (Hall, 2002). The economic crisis also revealed the existence of gaps in the unity of the European union members. During the crisis, nations failed to show a unified front and response in addressing the issue. Rather, there were divisions as each party seemed to pursue diverse and opposing strategies in addressing the issues. During the struggle to achieve economic stability, it was evident that countries, including France and Germany, were only in support of the European Union when it favoured their national interests and were against it when such was not the case.

The concept of globalisation has borne a substantial impact on nationalism among nations. While it aimed at broadening the human notion of a home, taking away the limited view of the home as one's country of origin or residence to the fact that a global home or county could exist. At such a time, however, nationalism seemed to prevail as each nation sought to protect whatever it believed in, forming associations and bodies that were tasked with looking after the interests of its citizens, even in the international arena. The psychological analysis of the conduct of nations in the face of globalization is considered compensatory (Ku and Yoo, 2013). If the feelings towards a home or a nation were rational, they could be broadened following the dynamics associated with globalisation. However, such feelings are limit-bound, thus triggering irrational responses among players and stakeholders in the global arena. The nostalgia associated with the home of feelings towards one's nation is considered projected feelings with nationalistic responses termed compensatory responses to the prevailing circumstances.

In the national arena, the psychological factors associated with the development of nationalism are associated with feelings of inferiority or resentment associated with national humiliation cases where a nation is defeated in its fight for national interest, it is likely to result in a radical transformation as nations seek to seal any gaps that led to their defeat (Walters, 2003). This arouses feelings towards collaboration and coordination of efforts for nationals to ensure unity and promotes nations towards pursuing their national interests.

In its extreme forms, nationalism is regarded as a cognitive disorder. Here, an individual's thought processes become concrete, and the metaphor of an individual's motherland becomes deeply ingrained in their conduct, behaviour, actions, and decisions. As such, individuals become devoid of their individuality as they become dissolved into the collective, societal ways of life. Consequently, the collective social minds take over the executive brain functions of an individual (Zmigrod, Rentfrow, and Robbins, 2018). As such, the individual cognitive faculties of the individual are now processed through the collective mind associated with the ancestral and subcortical functions of humanity, thus lacking adequate censorship. Under the influence of the collective mind, an individual is considered cognitively impaired, making decisions and acting based on the societal perspective rather than a rational individual rational mind.

Several propositions exist regarding nationalism and its impact on societies. Individuals' thoughts have equated nationalism to a mental disease such as OCD or alcoholism based on the consequences of nationalists' perceptions and thoughts on individuals and groups. While this may not be factual, people understand and try to explain the effect of nationalistic sentiments on the coexistence of people within national boundaries and the treatment of their mistreatment based on the concept of national identity. Consequently, nationalism is considered false esteem for fools. They are likely to use this concept to justify their actions against their fellow human beings by the mere division linked to their identities, which no one had a say in or could change. In some of the commentaries accessed towards this book's research, an individual point out the fear and delusion common among nationalist for no apparent and solid reasons. The commentator cannot place his hand on the reasons for such delusions and fear associated with nationalistic sentiments, saying that these emotions cannot be fully associated with ignorance (*R/Showerthoughts*).

A key factor in the conduct and behaviour of people in modern societies is associated with the concept of identity. The confusion associated with the concept is that the classifications need to be more solid and static. They change based on the diverse views and circumstances of the parties involved. Sometimes it could be division and violence along religious lines; other times, it is the origin of individuals and in some cases, just the belongingness to identified groups. It is, therefore, difficult to explain the reasons behind ethindividuals' violence. Nevertheless, these are not the only differentiating characteristics for individuals in a world characterised by differences associated with class, profession, gender, language, literature, science, and music, among others (Hauerwas, 2011). As global trends and organisations move towards managing such divisions, limitations exist due to the presumption of a singular and choiceless identity.

The concept of identity has proven difficult to explain while its impact is felt in societies across the globe. Shifting human attention to the fact that individuals share an identity with others raises the complications associated with equating an identity of individuals to oneself. The concept of identity influences various aspects of human lives through thoughts and actions, resulting in diverse views on political and contemporary social issues. The violence and atrocities visited upon the world in the past and those ongoing at the moment have resulted in terrible confusion and dreadful conflicts (Choi, 2022). The politics associated with this global confrontation is attributed to religious or cultural divisions existing in the world. This shows that the world is being perceived as a composition of religious federations and civilisations, ignoring how people perceive themselves. This line of thinking is based on the assumption that people in the world can be classified based on a single overarching system of partitioning, which is not true in the real world (Kaufmann, 1996).

The religious or civilisational partitioning of the world results in a solidaristic approach to human identity that considers human beings as members of exactly one group as defined by the differentiating approach selected. The approach leads to a misunderstanding of people and groups as people identified and classified into one group are expected to behave similarly, yet this is impossible to achieve. In normal human lives, individuals see themselves in a variety of broad divisions such as citizenship, place of residence, ancestry, Christianity or religious affiliations, way of life such as adherence to a vegetarian diet, and environmental and human rights activism, among such other classification without adversely influencing the overall conduct and interaction of individuals despite their unique classification along the identified differentiating characteristics. Each of the collectives identified above, together with many others not identified based on the numerous nature of likes, dislikes, and individual passions, gave them a sense of identity. Therefore, none of the identifying features can be taken and used as the only factor that can be used in dividing people into groups—such divisions in the past resulted in untold conflicts, suffering, and wars among individuals.

Adopting a classification system that led to the division of people based on religion resulted in mass conflicts between Muslims and other religious groups in India, as captured by Amartya Sen in his book *Identity and Violence*. He notes that violence is promoted by cultivating a sense of inevitability created by supposed identities, resulting in heavy demands being laid upon perceived group members. Such identities pave the way for sectarian confrontation as each group seeks to defend their members and their stand as regards any issues that could arise and cause divisions along various identifying features. Any well-intentioned efforts to stop such violence have been handicapped because individuals often lack choices regarding their identities. Once they have been classified based on their religious beliefs and outlooks, they are led to fight to maintain their beliefs without thinking of other features and factors that could bring them together, thus damaging humankind's ability to defeat violence.

Individuals' division and classification greatly damage the shared humanity's aspect into dominant classification systems, such as religions, communities, cultures, nations, or civilizations. There is a need for humans to understand the existing pluralities in human identity and the consequent appreciation that such differences cut across each other and work against the sharp separation of individuals along one hardened line of impenetrable division (Dahlsgaard, Peterson, and Seligman, 2005).

The illusions of destiny associated with singularity divisions of individuals have been considered the key contributing factor towards the turmoil and barbarity that characterise our world today. The illusion of density based on a particular identifying characteristic nurtures violence in the world through elements of omission or commission. Individuals need to see that they have many distinct affiliations and, therefore, can interact with each other differently. As such, individuals can decide on their priorities while interacting with others and appreciating the existing diversities within humanity.

Oscar Wilde, an Irish poet and playwright claimed that 'most people are other people' (Sen, 2001). While the statement seemed not to make sense at the moment, he defended that people's thoughts are, in most cases, other people's opinions of their lives a mimicry, and their passions identified and classified as quotations. This throws weight into the influence of identities and associations on human conduct, behaviour, and decisions (Yampolsky, Amiot, and de la Sablonnière, 2013). It is evident from this statement that people are greatly influenced by those with whom they identify. Consequently, when instigated by selfish leaders, a fostered sense of identity can be a powerful weapon for brutalising others.

Many conflicts within and outside nations are attributed to the illusion of a unique and choiceless identity that categorises individuals into groups. To create hatred between members of the identified groups, leaders invoke the powers of predominant identities such as religion, drowning any other affiliations that could have brought people together, allowing for collaboration and positive interaction for peaceful coexistence.

A sense of identity is a source of individuals' pride, joy, strength, and confidence. This idea has therefore received widespread admiration supporting and encouraging individuals to love their neighbours and extending to the adoption and implementation of high theories of social capital in societies. On the negative, the aspect of identity can kill! A sense of belonging to a group carries the perception of distance from other groups and individuals. Within-group solidarity has been cited for creating between-group discord. For example, the identities and classification of individuals result in the division of people within national boundaries (Hechter,1987). For example, even individuals with the same origin and identities can be classified based on their religious groups and affiliations, leading to divisions among them. In India, Martya notes that in the 1940s, political patriotism transformed broad human beings into fierce Muslims and ruthless Indians within just months! This resulted in the deaths of people in the hands of their people whom ruthless commanders had led to slaughter their own! He further noted that violence was fomented by the imposition of singular identities on gullible people and championed by artisans of terror without regard for the precious lives of the victims of such circumstances.

The sense of identity contributes significantly to the strengths and warmth in relationships with neighbours, fellow citizens, members of the community, as well as followers of the same religion. The aspects of identities are not negative in themselves, except that individuals use them negatively to create divisions among people. Human focus on particular identities is crucial for enriching bonds between people and helping people to do many things with each other while helping individuals to grow beyond their self-centred lives. The theory of social capital cites the crucial role of identity in the social community. It states that the concept of identity with others in communities is vital to improving livelihoods in communities (Lin, 2002). A sense of belongingness to a community is considered a crucial resource in human interactions and collaboration for collective community purposes.

On the other hand, it has been established that the sense of identity can exclude others even as it warmly embraces others. Consequently, it proposes that the sense of exclusion in communities based on predetermined classification criteria goes hand-in-hand with the gifts associated with inclusion. This, therefore, means that identities can be useful for bringing the good in societies on the one hand and breeding destruction on the other based on how members regard the acts.

The assumption of singular affiliation impacts human conduct and behaviour in association with others. It is clear that human beings are involved in identities of various kinds based on the prevailing contexts in their own lives, and that is considered to arise from their associations, backgrounds, or social activities. The same person can fall under several groups based on their country of residence, origin, interests, profession, lifestyle, and other differentiating features. This means that humans belong to many different groups in one way or another with each of the collectivises mentioned giving an individual a potentially different identity (Ludwick, 2016). For example, an individual can be grouped as a German citizen of British origin, a bodybuilder by profession, and a vegetarian by way of life with Indian racial characteristics. Here, individuals are left to determine their relevant identities from the various available options and weigh the importance of these different identities. The individual quoted above could decide whether the country of origin is more important than the country of residence or whether being a bodybuilder is more important than being of Chinese racial origin. It would be impossible to categorize the individual as Briton and expect them to support and adhere to the British features and conduct at all times, ignoring all the other differentiating features that make them human.

It is hard for theorists to justify the singular-affiliation view based on many differentiating characteristics and potential features for classifying people. Each individual patently belongs to many groups and classifications of human beings. It is, therefore, wrong to claim that despite the plurality of groups to which an individual potentially belongs, there is one that can explain the whole person. Therefore, the individual has no choice in deciding the relative importance of the different group memberships (Pani, 2011). The importance of the multitude of identities is based on the prevailing social contexts hence the choice of identities should be based on the contexts.

Additionally, not all human identities are of durable importance. Some exist for a season and vanish. It would also be crucial to note that not all characteristics or human features would be useful in creating a plausible basis for important group identity. For example, a group of people wearing the same shoe size may not be considered an ideal group with shared interests and features compared to individuals of the same origin. Once groups have been formed based on specified differentiating features, it acquires a derivative relevance, and this can be considered plausible enough for categorizing people into two separate groups.

An example of extremism in nationalistic sentiments is represented by the uproar in South Korea following the defeat of its skater Kim Yuna to a less experienced Russian. The uproar was characterised by millions of tweets protesting the game's outcomes. While thousands of sports officials globally could not understand the need for the uproar, it was evident that South Korea's reaction was based on the country's extremist feelings of nationalism towards themselves as evidenced by the feelings of competition against other players in the field. Sports fanaticism was associated with feelings towards others. The South Korean team considered itself superior to the others and could not justify nor accept the defeat. This expressed the nature and depth of nationalistic feelings among South Koreans, showcasing that such sentiments, associated with extremism, even war, could be perversive in the psychological aspects of humans as expressed in sports fandom. Nationalism makes people irrationally committed to one team so that if the team wins, people feel victorious and pleasure in other people's defeat (King, 2006).

From the social-psychological perspective, nationalist sentiments are attributed to attachment and identity. The above descriptions go hand in hand with the description of a nationalist as expressed by George Orwell. He notes that a nationalist uses their mental energy in either boosting or denigrating, thus focusing their mind on defeats, victories, humiliations, and triumphs. To a nationalist, the contemporary history of nations is considered the endless fall and rise of great power unions. Additionally, every event affecting nations demonstrates their capabilities and strengths, with one's nation being considered stronger or seeking to be stronger than its opponents. Nationalism is not equivalent to the mere worship of success.

On the contrary, the nationalist pozdes not simply gang up with the strongest side in history. Instead, a nationalist picks sides and persuades themselves that their side is superior to all the others. Thus, according to Orwell, nationalism is a power hunger combined with self-deception. Nationalists are capable of flagrant dishonesty and the thoughts of being in the right at all times.

Aspects of Nationalism

Even though all forms of nationalism are not similar, they have common factors and aspects that bring them together. Key among these is the aspect of obsession. Nationalists, wherever they are located across the globe, are obsessed with their power units. This is evidenced in their talk, thoughts, interactions with others, and writing. Nationalists cannot conceal their allegiance to their power units (Almog, 2013). A small criticism of their power units arouses a sense of uneasiness within a nationalist.

Similarly, praise of an opponent team arouses feelings of dislike for the person speaking, and the nationalist is likely to respond by making a sharp retort. If the opposing unit is a nation, the nationalist is more likely than not to showcase its superiority over the opponent in terms of military strength, political virtue, cooking, art, sport, literature, language, and physical beauty. In reality, one nation cannot be above others in all aspects, as stated above.

Another crucial feature of nationalists is instability. Their loyalties are transferable based on the presenting circumstances. Despite the changes in leaders and all other circumstances influencing the interaction between nations, the nationalist minds remain the same. They will support their power units despite their conduct and behaviours even if such is considered wrong by other players in the international arena. For a nationalist, the object of his feelings is changeable and may be imaginary (Davidson, 1993). Transferability allows nationalistic individuals to hold more to their nationalistic thoughts and ways of life. They are likely to be more vulgar, silly, malignant, and dishonest on behalf of their native countries.

Nationalistic individuals are also indifferent to reality. They have the power not to see the resemblance between similar sets of facts. Individuals are likely to defend self-determination in their nations without acknowledging the same in other nations under similar circumstances (Lieberman, 2021). For nationalists, actions are not considered wrong or immoral for what they are. Rather, their judgement depends on who does evil to them. Evil deeds such as the use of hostages, torture, mass deportations, child labour, assassination, forgery, and the bombing of civilians are greatly criticised when done by others yet are truly justifiable when carried out by one's nation is worth noting that nationalists are likely to approve the atrocities committed by its group with the increasing likelihood that they do not hear and share such experiences. It seems that people ignore the atrocities carried out by their group, assuming that they never existed and denying any knowledge of the existing and loud facts. For example, it would be hard for English people to acknowledge the extermination of the Polish and German Jews, yet the same seemed to have happened under their watch. In the nationalistic thinking process, thoughts are divided into the true and the untrue, as well as the known and the unknown. As such, a known fact could be unbearable that it is pushed aside and therefore not allowed to enter the logical processes. On the other hand, such thoughts could be acknowledged, entering into the various calculations for actions and decisions yet never admitted as facts in an individual's mind.

Nationalists are haunted by past occurrences with some wishing that such could be altered. Nationalist is more likely than not to spend more of their time in the fantasy world, seeking to build history by highlighting and considering those elements that support their national borders. The existing propagandist's writings are characterised by forgery where some material facts have been suppressed, alteration of dates have taken place, and quotations removed out of context to ensure that such writings are favourable for one's group. In building a nation's history, events that are felt not to have happened are denied and left unmentioned in a nation's literature.

Among nationalists also exist an element of indifference to the objective truth. Here, individuals are increasingly likely to seal off one part of the world from another, making it hard for individuals and leaders to know and discover what is happening. It results in genuine doubt regarding even the most enormous events, including the fact that calamities such as massacres, revolutions, famines, and battles are likely to inspire an average person toward feelings of unreality. Additionally, nationalism makes it difficult for an individual to verify the facts based on the adoption of different presentations and representations based on the side one supports and fights for in such occurrences. The general uncertainty associated with such occurrences makes it easier for individuals and leaders to stick to their lunatic beliefs. In nationalistic occurrences, it is quite impossible to prove or disapprove of certain occurrences. Then it is easier for individuals to deny such events prudently. All that matters to a nationalist is that he/she wants their unit to get better and outperform other units by scoring off the adversaries without examining the facts. Consequently, all nationalistic controversies are often inconclusive as each contestant believes they have won as opposed to their opponents (Mosse, 1987).

Research relates nationalism to the emotion of disgust. The emotion causes more negative attitudes as exhibited by a group to the outgroups while treating them in groups with favour. Consequently, nationalism has been regarded as a conservative concept with negative intergroup values. Although this emotion was in the past associated with a reaction towards negative stimuli, it has evolved to become an element for the rejection of outsiders by existing self-protecting systems such as nations or identified groups of individuals. In this sense, outgroup individuals are considered a source of contamination to a specified nation or group (Dekker, Malová, and Hoogendoorn, 2003).

Consequently, there is an increased likelihood for a nation to consider outsiders with prejudice and negative attitudes similar to the disease-avoidance function of disgust. Research has shown that chronic and negative feelings associated with the treatment of outsiders have been the key motivating factor for xenophobic feelings and attitudes toward foreigners. In another research, it was established that a relationship existed between disease avoidance and ethnocentrisms. The higher the level of disgust sensitivity, the stronger the ethnocentric feelings among the studied groups.

Nationalism is considered a crucial factor detrimental to group evaluations. It promotes the feeling that one's country is superior to others and should therefore dominate over the rest. Nationalism is reported to emphasise the need for national purity, which cannot be easily attained, especially due to rising globalization. Other critical factors of nationalism include national power and national self-determination. These are the same features affecting ethnocentrisms and featured in the diverse levels of disgust witnessed in such societal settings. Disgust is also associated with power-seeking behaviours as exhibited among nationalists. In some circumstances, it has been established that disgust leads to the pursuit of cultural and religious purity, helping specified groups from being contaminated by outgroup pathogens. The feelings of disgust among nationalists and other self-seeking groups also contribute significantly to the accessibility to death-related thoughts. Such thoughts, according to the terror-management theory, motivate individuals towards the pursuit of power in order to protect their psychological security.

The Concept of Identity and Cognitive Theories

According to cognitive development theorists, children go through socialisation processes as they grow from egocentric to socio-centric, building attachments to groups based on the need to fulfil their basic human needs. The aspects of attachment and identity, therefore, permeate all acts of human interactions and influence behaviour and individual conduct in the face of circumstances that call for the choosing or supporting of a team or a side in various spheres of life. At national levels, nations are supported based on the fact that they fulfil the economic, political, and socio-cultural needs of individuals giving them prestige and the feeling of belonging (Brubaker, 2009). This explains the reactions witnessed in the Olympic games and South Korea's extreme reaction to the loss. Consequently, psychological schools of thought agree that humans consider belonging a fundamental basic need. National attachment is thought to fulfil that needs and help individuals construct their identity.

Identity-based thinking is subject to brutal manipulation by leaders who want to recruit individuals into hating others who are considered outsiders to specified groups. Individuals need to understand and appreciate the broad commonality of shared humanity while recognising the preservation of identities that could be common among individuals yet have been left out among nationalists (Akerlof, 2016). Hence, others ways of people classification can emerge, restraining the possibility of exploitation of specifically aggressive approaches to particular and common categorisations.

The cognitive illusion associated with the broad singular categorisation of people into two groups has received well-mentioned and disastrous support from practitioners and theorists who consider community identity crucial to human survival (Cohen and Lefebvre, 2005). On the other hand, cultural theorists are likely to partition people into little boxes composed of disparate civilisations. In normal human lives, various factors play a role in determining an individual relative of their belongingness. Individuals are considered members of diverse groups, including their citizenship, geographic origin, class, and gender. Employment status, habits, sports interests, and social commitments make them members of various groups. Each of these existing collectivities in which people simultaneously belong informs their particular identities. There is no way only one of these aspects can be used to define individuals while castigating those that do not belong to the specified groups.

Charged attributions common in nationalistic and divisive politics are characterised by two interrelated distortions: the inadequate and incorrect description of people and the insistence that the ascribed features are the only major features that describe the groups. Degradation of individuals is attributed to the descriptive misrepresentation and the singular identity that individuals must attribute to the person to be demeaned (Maling and O'Connor, 2015). Organised attribution of individuals prepares the ground through which people are persecuted and mistreated in societies due to the group and national conflicts.

Nationalism and Human Rights

Nationalism emerged as an ideology that promised to protect the rights of citizens against the monarchs. It later turned into an ideology used by rulers, leaders, and political actors to justify human rights violations. It is evident from the preceding research in the area that nationalism has been considered inherently contradictory to human rights. Nationalism applies preference order, in which individuals within national boundaries are grouped and treated based on the ordering features and characteristics. Here, the nationalist political leaders seek to achieve and protect national unity at any cost while prioritising the interest of the nation over those of its citizens. The need to achieve such goals jeopardizes various human rights, including the freedom of association and assembly, speech, and electoral determination as these rights can be applied to challenging national unity (Yazici, 2019). Additionally, research indicates that national governments are reckless in using force, torture, extrajudicial killings, and political improvements to keep societies and individuals in check.

One of the key negative elements of nationalism, as regards human rights, is the tendency of the concept to violate individuals' rights through violence, including ethnic conflicts and genocides. In some cases, it has been established that leaders of ethnic groups who are aware that conflicts in certain areas are likely to increase the solidarity of members of a specified ethnic group have instigated such ethnic conflicts to achieve their desired objectives—unity within an ethnic community. As such, ethnic nationalism has been linked with one of the most violent forms of human rights violations (Exdell, 2009). While civic nationalism has been cited as more protective of human rights than its ethnic nationalism counterpart, research shows that the outcomes are not as presumed. Civic nationalism also prioritises the interest of the majority over minority groups at the expense of individual rights. This results in the likelihood of civic nationalism coercing minority cultures into being part of a homogenous nation, thus suppressing the interest of these groups. This outcome amounts to the engendering of human rights violations, especially as it touches on the rights of minority groups.

Research shows that the main components of nationalism: national identity, autonomy, and unity, engender specific security and social policy prescriptions by informing national preference orderings. The constant pursuit of national unity among governments results in the repression of minorities and the consequent violation of empowerment rights among such groups. This limits the freedom of speech, association and assembly, and electoral self-determination, especially affecting minority groups. As they design legislation and policies targeted toward social events and occurrences, there is an increasing likelihood that nationalist governments are likely to be intolerant and aggressive towards any group that is likely to challenge national unity (Triandafyllidou, 1998). Thus, the primary tension associated with nationalism lies in the need for self-determination and how much is achieved while considering the concerns and interests of all citizens within the national borders. As nationalist governments seek national unity, it is apparent that they may not be willing to grant electoral determination as a right to the minority groups over their majority counterparts. Even in cases where nationalism does not oppose the freedom of association and speech among its citizens, it has, in some instances, suspended those rights when they seem to affect the state of unity in the nations adversely.

Prioritisation of collective over individual interest has been cited as a major factor affecting human rights in nationalistic governments. Such practices as extrajudicial killings, political imprisonment, torture, and disappearance have been reported, especially among dissenting voices in governance processes. Some governments have been forced to choose between individual and national interests. For example, security forces within national boundaries may apply force and torture in gathering intelligence as they seek to fight elements of espionage and terrorist threats in the nations. In response to protest movements, national governments have often tortured the protesters to deter other individuals from getting involved in such events. While politically liberal governments may prioritise the rights of individuals and apply peaceful means in handling issues affecting their citizens, nationalist governments often cite national security as the main reason for suspending human rights despite any element of criticism that could arise within the international community (Yazici, 2019). Nationalist governments may also imprison people due to non-violent political acts that could threaten national unity and security.

In addressing human rights in nationalist governance, it is vital to know that sometimes policymakers are convinced that human rights could be violated to aid in achieving the nation's ideological goals. In some cases, however, policymakers seem to take advantage of the elusiveness of national interest and security concepts to justify their actions. However, such is intended to ensure political survival without regard for the nation's well-being.

Nationalism and Xenophobia

A report by the United Nations Human Rights Office indicates that the world seems to have returned to an era where the unjustifiable fear of others, socially those considered as outsiders-including immigrants and refugees, seems to have been normalised. It seems from the report that the politicians are at the forefront, blaming these individuals and groups of people for the failures reported in the security and economic spheres of governance. Politicians have blamed the increasing movement of immigrants and refugees into their countries as the main cause of issues and challenges facing their nations, resulting in cases of abuse, hate speech, violence, and prejudice against them (Bordeau, 2009).

In the political arena, electoral campaigns have been seen to use xenophobic utterances and discourses to mobilise its citizens towards supporting policies that address the challenges. Using such strategies goes against the democratic principles that should govern nations, as well as the need to observe the human rights of all people despite their positions and perceived importance in the nation. This has resulted in extreme and narrow nationalism characterised by scapegoating and stigmatising perceived foreigners, thus leading to the exclusion of certain people from the protection of the law (Thorleifsson, 2018). The silence by states in addressing such instances and occurrences is linked to the growth of xenophobic and racist utterances that result in the discrimination and racist treatment of individuals based on their national origin and migratory status. It is considered wrong for a nation to justify the vilification of minority groups who are made to carry the burden of societal failures just because they are considered outsiders in specific national boundaries.

In extreme cases, organised and vigilante groups have been formed and supported by the political elites to expel migrants and refugees from their communities based on the narrow definition of nationalism and the exclusion of such individuals from the classification. As a result of such a classification of individuals, leaders have designed legislative initiatives to ban certain dress codes and associate certain groups of people with terrorism. Additionally, instances of the incompatibility of cultural minorities with the values and principles of the nation have been cited, thus discriminating against those minority groups in providing services and equal rights to all people within one's national boundaries (Laryš, 2019). The United Nations representative, in his argument, notes that world leaders should commit themselves to condemning political leaders and parties that base their campaign platforms on the stigmatisation of minorities, migrants, and refugees while providing leadership vital for the protection of such vulnerable groups in societies. There is a need for political leaders to condemn and counter any political messages that fuel racism and xenophobia (United Nations, 2016).

Anti-migrant narratives seem to point out the negatives and disadvantages of opening up a county's borders to foreigners. When pursued to the extreme, such beliefs are likely to result in prejudice, discrimination, and the violation of the human rights of the minority groups based on their descent and other features that distinguish them from the aboriginal groups. Some anti-immigrant policies perpetuate the false assumption that migrants take away from their communities of destination something that rightfully belongs to the citizens (Hjerm, 2001). As such, they propose that sharing the aboriginal culture and country with the immigrant population results in losses for the aboriginal population. This argument is not right as the people migrating to another nation have something to offer in return for the hospitality received from such nations. However, research also shows the critical contribution of migrants and refugees to their countries of destination in the form of economic and developmental aspects of the community.

In seeking to defend instances of discrimination against minority groups such as immigrants and refugees, various researchers have studied citizens' attitudes towards such movements. In seeking to explain the opposition of Americans to legal immigration, it was established that citizens looked at the impact of such movements on the economic and other interests of American citizens. Instead of opposing immigration as a dislike for the immigrants specifically, it was established that the Americans were opposed to the concept based on their desire to serve and defend the interest of American citizens as regards access to services and employment opportunities that would be shared equally by both the citizens and the non-citizens (Neocosmos, 2010). Here, Americans were more likely to express political favouritism towards their fellow citizens based on shared citizenship. The major concept for the policy and decision makers lay on whether immigrants would harm or not cause any harm to the American citizens.

The research also showed that the citizens held elements of discrimination and prejudice against immigrants and refugees. The survey showed that American citizens considered immigrants, both legal and illegal, as impoverished, hurting the economy by driving down wages or increasing unemployment rates, thus affecting the well-being of American citizens. It is critical to note that nationalism, just like xenophobia, is irrational concept that seeks to judge individuals based on elements they have no control (Kecmanovic, 2005). Opponents of nationalism and xenophobia feel that an individual's residence, represented by a position on the map, should bear no influence on their humanity. While xenophobia is considered as antipathy towards individuals one has never met based on the fact that they live outside the borders of one's country, then nationalism can be cited as the sympathy one feels towards others one has never met yet living within a nation's borders.

Rationally, it would suffice to say that the same treatment should be meted on the two classes classified above. Yet classifications are made based on their belonging or otherwise to the nation. To the nationalist, however, people living within the arbitrary boundaries of the nation deserve to have their interests protected by the national states even at the expense of the interest of those that live outside those boundaries. No logical explanations can be used to justify the situation as such actions are based on the emotional aspects of the situation. Such irrationality is almost invisible as nationalism is considered part of one's cultural background, which is hard to notice. Individuals are raised watching the news, learning their nation's history, and associating with individuals within their national boundaries (Gerber, 2014). Such association is so natural that we tend to defend those with whom we share similar ideas, norms, ideologies, and concepts. The issue arises when another is discriminated against or prejudiced against. However, they have no say in their countries of origin, status, residence, and other such differentiating features that inform the fair treatment of others on the one hand and the discrimination and unfair treatment of others on the other. Such tendencies often lead to the belief that one's country should therefore address the needs of its citizens first without having all individuals within the borders enjoy the same rights as the aboriginal population groups.

It is worth noting that borders that leaders and citizens take for granted and that form the foundation of politics and policies are artificial. These borders are considered historical contingencies with little significance yet have been obeyed and observed insignificantly based on the culture's preoccupation with the people living within such borders. Political analysts have varying views regarding the treatment and perspectives on borders. On the extreme of the divide, some philosophers seem to encourage individuals to think of themselves as citizens of the worldwide community of human beings. However, others state that it would be difficult to justify the position of nation-states in conferring great advantages to individuals based on their births. Nevertheless, restrictions are made regarding the free movement of people across national boundaries (Barrow, 2017).

Nationalism—the Measles of Mankind

Nationalism is considered a state of mind through which one perceives messages regarding one's nation, images, and memories regarding the preferred status in all respects. It is considered a concept that spreads its influence across the globe—permeating every aspect of individual and societal lives (O'Leary, 2001). Its comparison to measles is linked to how the concept is visible and evidenced in various spheres of human life. It leaves its legacy across cultures while becoming an embarrassment to the prevailing political philosophies across nations. This is associated with the harms associated with the concept in the local and international arena in the form of bloodshed, property destruction, and displacement of people. These have been exhibited and characterised through civil wars and the variations of ethnic cleansing across the globe. However, people are to learn and therefore defend and prevent such actions from occurring. How nationalism has spread across Europe and the world at large gives it the comparison to measles, a contagious disease for humankind. Key among the concepts of nationalism include the emancipation and oppression of individuals who are considered outsiders and foreigners in one's nation (Haidt, 2016). Nevertheless, more confusing is that nationalism permeates every part of human nature, enabling an individual to value their past and treasure the factors and elements common among all the citizens within identified national borders. On the other hand, such a way of thinking points out the differences that exist between them, thus resulting in instances where different kind of treatment is meted upon outgroups as compared to ingroups.

Nationalism is further considered a disease because it breeds sectarianism in societies resulting in conflicts characterised by violence and civil wars. Nationalism adversely affects rational decision-making in politics resulting in leaders who make decisions without due regard to the diverse needs of their population. Focus on cultural aspects of nationalism tends for people to remain imprisoned in the past and primitive ways even though contemporary society is dynamic and ever-changing. As individuals seek to defend their interests and maintain their sense of esteem and dignity, the evils of nationalism have heavily been felt in civil wars. This disease is characterised by the tendency of individuals to fight against others based on their different and sometimes opposing ideologies and belief systems. Such group behaviour features insularity and exclusivity, thus fuelling hostility towards rival groups.

Brain Anatomy and Nationalism

In 2016, Takeuchi et al completed a study in which they tried to determine the brain structure differences associated with patriotism and nationalism. The results were stunning. Nationalism was associated with neurocognitive mechanisms in social-related areas and limbic neural areas while patriotism is mediated by neurocognitive mechanisms in areas related to well-being. What do all these findings mean? Well, the fact that nationalism is associated with the limbic system indicated that nationalism is a product of the emotional, irrational, fearful part of the brain.

There is a saying, keep it frontal don't go limbic! There is a very good reason for it. The frontal and prefrontal cortexes are the ones that separate us from reptiles and other animals. They make us humans, rational, loving, and caring creatures. On the other hand, the limbic system, the core of nationalism is situated in the middle of the brain and is involved in emotional responses, learning and creating memories. It is also called the paleomammalian cortex for this reason. This part of the brain is responsible for 'us versus them'. Survival behaviour is its primal function (fear, arousal, and psychosomatic response). It is not difficult to make a conclusion that nationalism is a product of an irrational and impulsive part of the brain. I will try to keep it very simple and without going into too many details I will plainly explain how different parts of the limbic system works and why they are associated with nationalism.

The limbic system is made of the amygdala, hippocampus, hypothalamus, thalamus, and cingulate gyrus, and it is situated in the middle of our brain. If we could imagine a line between our hearts and another one in between our eyes, the limbic system will be at the point where those two lines are crossing.

Amygdala is a small almond-shaped part of the limbic system designed to process fearful and threatening stimuli and activate psychosomatic responses in life-threatening or dangerous situations. It is responsible for negative emotions and thoughts as well as for the fight or flight response. Hippocampus has a major role in learning and memory. The thalamus is a consciousness and senses-related station. Hypothalamus is responsible for the balance-like state in our body called homeostasis. In order to keep our body in the perfect balance, it has control over our hormones. And finally, the cingulate gyrus helps regulate emotions and pain in our body. All reptiles have a limbic system in their brains. It is a primitive part of the brain. Now we can easily see the correlation between nationalism and self-destruction in humans.

Conclusion

Research into nationalism showcases the existence of various theories that seek to explain the behaviour of a group vis-à-vis their treatment of its members and outsiders. Various factors including our brain structure and cognitive or thinking patterns contribute to the behaviour of people classified as residents of a nation-state. On the one hand, it is logical to explain the kind of bond between people classified as having a common identity based on the features and characteristics between them. It is challenging to define and explain the existence of differences and conflicts between different groups, yet the differentiating features are considered circumstantial as opposed to permanent factors. Thus, the chapter explains the elements of national identity and self, the likelihood for people to pursue extreme and negative views against others and thus react in the form of wars and xenophobia, resulting in further conflicts between people from diverse national boundaries. Such occurrences significantly impact the various aspects of human lives, as explained by their exacerbation of wars and the possible loss of lives and property. Thus, researchers try to point out that the concept of nationalism has been used by nations, especially those that consider themselves superior to others, as a means through which they seek to pursue their interests at the expanse of all others. The resulting conflicts are further fuelled by the fact that each nation seeks to maintain its superiority at all costs even if it means engaging in military attacks against opponents. There is a need, however, to pursue the interests of all humanity based on the fact that the existing differentiating features are superficial and ever-changing rather than stable and fixed in nature.

References

Abrams, D and Hogg, M A (2010) 'Social Identity and Self-Categorization', *The SAGE handbook of Prejudice, Stereotyping and Discrimination*, pp 179–93.

Akerlof, R (2016) '"We Thinking" and Its Consequences', *American Economic Review*, 106(5), pp 415–19.

Allen, M J (2017) 'From Humiliation to Human Rights', *Reviews in American History*, 45(1), pp 159–166.

Almog, O (2013) 'Shifting the Centre from Nation to Individual and Universe: The New "Democratic Faith" of Israel', *Israel: The First Hundred Years*. Routledge, pp 31–42.

Barrow, E (2017) 'No global citizenship? Re-envisioning global citizenship education in times of growing nationalism', *The High School Journal*, 100(3), pp 163–165.

Baumeister, R F (2001) 'Violent pride', *Scientific American*, 284(4), 96–101.

Bechhofer, F and McCrone, D (2009) 'National identity, nationalism and constitutional change', *National Identity, Nationalism and Constitutional Change*. Palgrave Macmillan, London, pp 1–16.

Bordeau, J (2009) *Xenophobia*. The Rosen Publishing Group, Inc.

Brading, D A (1994) 'Nationalism and state-building in Latin American history', *Ibero-Amerikanisches Archiv*, 20(1/2), pp 83–108.

Breuer, J and Elson, M (2017) *Frustration-Aggression Theory*. Wiley Blackwell, pp 1–12.

Britt, L and Heise, D (2000) 'From shame to pride in identity politics', *Self, Identity, and Social Movements*, 5, pp 252–268.

Brubaker, R (2009) 'Ethnicity, race, and nationalism', *Annual Review of Sociology*, pp 21–42.

Buttle, N (2000) 'Critical nationalism: a liberal prescription?', *Nations and Nationalism*, 6(1), pp 111–127.

Charkawi, W, Dunn, K, and Bliuc, A M (2021) 'The influences of social identity and perceptions of injustice on support to violent extremism', *Behavioral Sciences of Terrorism and Political Aggression*, 13(3), pp 177–196.

Charney, E (2003) 'Identity and liberal nationalism', *American Political Science Review*, 97(2), pp 295–310.

Choi, S W (2022) 'Leader nationalism, ethnic identity, and terrorist violence', *British Journal of Political Science*, 52(3), pp 1151–1167.

Cohen, H and Lefebvre, C (eds) (2005) *Handbook of Categorization in Cognitive Science*. Elsevier.

Coller, X. (2006) 'Collective identities and failed nationalism', *Pôle Sud*, (2), pp 107–136.

Dahlsgaard, K, Peterson, C, and Seligman, M E (2005) 'Shared virtue: The convergence of valued human strengths across culture and history', *Review of General Psychology*, 9(3), pp 203–213.

Davidson, B (1993) *The Black Man's Burden: Africa and the Curse of the Nation-State*. Times Press.

De Vries, C E and Van Kersbergen, K (2007) 'Interests, identity and political allegiance in the European Union', *Acta Politica*, 42(2), pp 307–328.

Dekker, H, Malová, D, and Hoogendoorn, S (2003) 'Nationalism and its explanations', *Political Psychology*, 24(2), pp 345–376.

Dekker, H., Malová, D, and Hoogendoorn, S (2003) 'Nationalism and its explanations', *Political Psychology*, 24(2), pp 345–376.

Dinan, D. (Ed.). (2014). *Origins and evolution of the European Union.* Oxford University Press.

Duckitt, J (2005) 'Personality and prejudice', *On the Nature of Prejudice: Fifty Years after Allport*, pp 395–412.

Etherington, J (2010) 'Nationalism, territoriality and national territorial belonging', *Papers: Revista de Sociologia*, pp 321–339.

Exdell, J (2009) 'Immigration, nationalism, and human rights', *Metaphilosophy*, 40(1), pp 131–146.

Triandafyllidou, A (1998) 'National identity and the "other"', *Ethnic and Racial Studies*, 21(4), pp 593–612.

Fabrykant, M and Magun, V (2016) 'Grounded and normative dimensions of national pride in comparative perspective', *Dynamics of National Identity: Media and Societal Factors of What We Are*, pp 109–138.

Fabrykant, M and Magun, V (2019) 'Dynamics of National Pride Attitudes in Post-Soviet Russia, 1996–2015', *Nationalities Papers*, 47(1), pp 20–37.

Fearon, J D and Laitin, D D (2000) 'Violence and the social construction of ethnic identity', *International Organization*, 54(4), pp 845–877.

Ferguson, N and McAuley, J W (2021) 'Dedicated to the cause: Identity development and violent extremism', *European Psychologist*, 26(1), p 6.

Gerber, T P (2014) 'Beyond Putin? Nationalism and xenophobia in Russian public opinion', *The Washington Quarterly*, 37(3), pp 113–134.

Gong, L (2007) 'Ethnic identity and identification with the majority group: Relations with national identity and self-esteem', *International Journal of Intercultural Relations*, 31(4), pp 503–523.

Gray, K A (2005) 'Pride, prejudice, and a dose of shame: The meaning of public assistance', *Affilia*, 20(3), pp 329–345.

Hall, R C (2002) *The Balkan Wars 1912–1913: Prelude to the First World War*. Routledge.

Hauerwas, S (2011) *War and the American Difference: Theological Reflections on Violence and National Identity*. Baker Academic.

Hechter, M (1987) *Principles of Group Solidarity*, vol 11. University of California Press.

Hjerm, M (2001) Education, xenophobia and nationalism: A comparative analysis', *Journal of Ethnic and Migration Studies*, 27(1), pp 37–60.

Hogg, M A (2007) 'Uncertainty–identity theory', *Advances in Experimental Social Psychology*, 39, pp 69–126.

Hogg, M A and Adelman, J (2013) 'Uncertainty–identity theory: Extreme groups, radical behavior, and authoritarian leadership', *Journal of Social Issues*, 69(3), pp 436–454.

Hornsey, M J (2008) 'Social identity theory and self-categorization theory: A historical review', *Social and Personality Psychology Compass*, 2(1), pp 204–222.

Jáuregui, P (2000) 'National pride and the meaning of 'Europe': a comparative study of Britain and Spain', *The Sociological Review*, 48(1_suppl), pp 257–287.

Kaufmann, C (1996) 'Possible and impossible solutions to ethnic civil wars', *International Security*, 20(4), pp 136–175.

Kecmanovic, D (2005) 'The rational and the irrational in nationalism', *Studies in Ethnicity and Nationalism*, 5(1), pp 2–26.

King, A (2006) 'Nationalism and sport', *The Sage Handbook of Nations and Nationalism*. London: Sage, pp 249–259.

Ku, J and Yoo, J (2013) 'Globalization and sovereignty', *Berkeley J. Int'l L.*, 31, 210.

Landau, H (2020) 'Economic and Political Nationalism and Private Foreign Investments', *Denver Journal of International Law and Policy*, 2(2), p 3.

Laryš, M (2019) 'Violent attacks against migrants and minorities in the Russian federation', *Vigilantism against Migrants and Minorities*. Routledge, pp 69–85.

Lieberman, B (2021) 'From Nationalism to National Indifference: Binary Logic and Sense of Time', *Nationalities Papers*, 49(5), pp 855–872.

Lin, N (2002) *Social Capital: A Theory of Social Structure and Action*, vol 19. Cambridge University Press.

Ludwick, K W (2016) *The Legend of the Lone Wolf: Categorizing Singular and Small Group Terrorism* (doctoral dissertation, George Mason University).

Ma, S Y (1992) 'Nationalism: State-building or state-destroying?', *The Social Science Journal*, 29(3), pp 293–305.

Machida, S (2012) 'Does globalization render people more ethnocentric? Globalization and people's views on cultures', *The American Journal of Economics and Sociology*, 71(2), pp 436–469.

Maling, J and O'Connor, C (2015) 'Cognitive illusions: non-promotional passives and unspecified subject constructions', *Structures in the Mind: Essays on Language, Music, and Cognition in Honor of Ray Jackendoff*, pp 101–118.

Mansbridge, J J (ed) (1990) *Beyond Self-Interest*. University of Chicago Press.

Margalit, A and Raz, J (1990) National self-determination', *The Journal of Philosophy*, 87(9), pp 439–461.

Medrano, J D and Gutiérrez, P (2001) 'Nested identities: national and European identity in Spain', *Ethnic and Racial Studies*, 24(5), pp 753–778.

Mosse, G L (1987) *Masses and Man: Nationalist and Fascist Perceptions of Reality*. Wayne State University Press.

Neocosmos, M (2010) 'From Foreign Natives to Native Foreigners. Explaining Xenophobia in Post-Apartheid South Africa: Explaining Xenophobia', *Post-Apartheid South Africa: Citizenship and Nationalism, Identity and Politics*. African Books Collective.

Nussbaum, M (1994) 'Patriotism and cosmopolitanism', *The Cosmopolitan Reader*, pp 155–162.

O'Leary, B (2001) 'An iron law of nationalism and federation?: A (neo-Diceyian) theory of the necessity of a federal Staatsvolk, and of consociational rescue', *Nations and Nationalism*, 7(3), pp 273–296.

Ostrowsky, M K (2010) 'Are violent people more likely to have low self-esteem or high self-esteem?', *Aggression and Violent Behavior*, 15(1), pp 69–75.

Pani, N (2011) 'Identity and political choice: the co-existence of singular affiliation politics and pluralism', *Contemporary Politics*, 17(1), pp 35–52.

Pei, M (2003) 'The paradoxes of American nationalism', *Foreign Policy*, pp 31–37.

R/Showerthoughts—'Nationalism' Is the Same Mental Illness an Alcoholism but Extroverted Instead of Introverted (nd). Reddit. https://www.reddit.com/r/Showerthoughts/comments/b23ukb/nationalism_is_the_same_mental_illness_an/.

Reeskens, T and Wright, M (2013) 'Nationalism and the cohesive society: A multilevel analysis of the interplay among diversity, national identity, and social capital across 27 European societies', *Comparative Political Studies*, 46(2), pp 153–181.

Reicher, S and Hopkins, N (2000) *Self and Nation*. Sage.

Risse, T (2002) 'Nationalism and Collective Identities. Europe versus the Nation-State?', *Developments in West European Politics*, 2, pp 77–93.

Sen, A (2001, January) 'Other people', *Proceedings-British Academy*, vol 111. Oxford University Press Inc, pp. 319–338.

Sidanius, J and Pratto, F (2012) 'Social dominance theory', *Handbook of Theories of Social Psychology*, 2.

Solberg, C (2021) 'Immigration and nationalism', *Immigration and Nationalism*. University of Texas Press.

Solt, F (2011) 'Diversionary nationalism: Economic inequality and the formation of national pride', *The Journal of Politics*, 73(3), pp 821–830.

Spinner-Halev, J and Theiss-Morse, E (2003) 'National identity and self-esteem', *Perspectives on Politics*, 1(3), pp. 515–532.

Stephens, W, Sieckelinck, S, and Boutellier, H (2021) 'Preventing violent extremism: A review of the literature', *Studies in Conflict and Terrorism*, 44(4), pp 346–361.

Takeuchi, H, Taki, Y, Sekiguchi, A, *et al* (2016) 'Differences in gray matter structure correlated to nationalism and patriotism', *Sci Rep* **6**, 29912. https://doi.org/10.1038/srep29912.

Thorleifsson, C (2018) *Nationalist Responses to the Crises in Europe: Old and New Hatreds*. Routledge.

Tilley, J and Heath, A (2007) 'The decline of British national pride 1', *The British Journal of Sociology*, 58(4), pp 661–678.

United Nations (2016, September) *The Spectre of Nationalistic and Xenophobic Politics Looms over Migrants and Refugees*. OHCHR. https://www. ohchr.org/en/stories/2016/09/spectre-nationalistic-and-xenophobic-politics-looms-over-migrants-and-refugees.

Velotti, P, Garofalo, C, Bottazzi, F, and Caretti, V (2017) 'Faces of shame: Implications for self-esteem, emotion regulation, aggression, and well-being', *The Journal of Psychology*, 151(2), pp 171–184.

Walter, B F (2017) 'The extremist's advantage in civil wars', *International Security*, 42(2), pp 7–39.

Walters, R W (2003) *White Nationalism, Black Interests: Conservative Public Policy and the Black Community*. Wayne State University Press.

Wimmer, A and Glick Schiller, N (2002) 'Methodological nationalism and beyond: nation–state building, migration and the social sciences', *Global Networks*, 2(4), pp 301–334.

Yampolsky, M A, Amiot, C E, and de la Sablonnière, R (2013) 'Multicultural identity integration and well-being: A qualitative exploration of variations in narrative coherence and multicultural identification', *Frontiers in Psychology*, 4, 126.

Yazici, E (2019) 'Nationalism and human rights', *Political Research Quarterly*, 72(1), pp 147–161.

Zapotoczny, W S 'National Pride and National Positioning Made World War I Inevitable'.

Zmigrod, L, Rentfrow, P J, and Robbins, T W (2018) 'Cognitive underpinnings of nationalistic ideology in the context of Brexit', *Proceedings of the National Academy of Sciences*, 115(19), E4532-E4540.

Putin, Vladimir 35

R

racism 23, 54, 69, 91, 137
radical nationalism 23-4
reactionary nationalism 22-3
realism 99-100, 102, 128
realism theory 99
realists, structural 101, 119
religious-based nationalism 91
religious nationalism 21, 48
revolutions 26
    liberal nationalist 22
Robinson, Thomas W. 96
Roman Empire 26, 31, 90
Russia 34, 113
Rwanda 75

S

sacrifice, readiness to 2-3
sacrifices, readiness to 6
Savannah principle 63
Schweickart, Rusty 53
Searle-White, Joshua 56-7, 79
secondary interests 96
self-categorisation 138-9
self-determination, national 22, 29, 159, 173
self-esteem iii, ix, 61, 72, 131, 134-5, 145-6, 171, 175
self-identity 72, 134
self-respect 135-6, 145
Sen, Amartya 152
Serbia 13
Serbian 12
Serbs 13, 24
shared morality 70
slave morality 71
Slovenia 13
Smith, Anthony 31
social agents 75-6

social categorization 80
social coordination 76
social decision scheme 74
social identity theory 61, 72, 79-80, 138, 172
social influence 73
societies 10
    constitutional democratic 103
    emancipated 20
    liberal 103
solidarity, within-group 154
South Korea 156, 160
sovereignty 9, 12, 47, 103, 106, 124-6, 135
    absence of 12
    national 17, 32, 147
Soviet Union 28, 35, 95
stability, economic 122, 150
states 11-13, 17, 102, 113
    liberal 102-4, 136
    purpose of existence 12
states system 105-7
stereotyping 58, 72, 169
substate nationalists 29
Sukarno (founding father) 32
system, limbic 66, 167-8

T

Tajfel, Henri 61, 72, 74, 80
territorial nationalism 21
terror management theory 54, 77
terrorism 41-2, 51, 136, 164, 170, 173, 175
    international 98
thalamus 168
Tolstoy (Russian writer) 9
traits 7, 13, 55, 69-70, 98
tunnel vision, of reality 69
Tversky, Amos 118

9 798369 490174